Hen... ...oliday

From

Hell

Chapter 1

Forty year old Henry Pratt was no 'Jack the Lad'; in fact he was more than content with being a 'Jack in the Corner' who exhibited an uncanny ability to melt into any number of backgrounds with ease. He wore 'conservative' clothes and sensible shoes. His receding hair was 'styled' short back and sides and he hadn't a clue as to the intricacies of football's 'offside rule'.

He was, it must also be said, something of a first class nerd.

He had excelled at school before gaining a good university degree in Chemistry; but unfortunately, his personal lack of drive and 'chemistry' ended up guiding him onto a career path that took him to the dizzying heights of a product development manager at a large soap powder manufacturing company in Trafford Park, Manchester... and he was quite content with his lot...that is, until one day, he ran into Maximilian (Max for short) Power.

Maximilian was everything that he, Henry was not. He wore 'cool threads, he was about 6'2" to Henry's 5' 6"(ish). He had a pony tail, a diamond earring, a thousand

Watt £20,000 orthodontics augmented smile and a degree of self confidence that relegated Christiano Ronaldo and Zlatan Ibrahimovic into the shrinking violet category. He was also a new hot shot PR manager. And on his very first day at work, his 'I am the dog's bollocks' attitude got right up Henry's hooter.

"Who does he think he is; parading around like he's God's Gift," Henry muttered to himself in the staff canteen where 'Max', who was sat at a nearby table of giggling young women who seemed to hang on his every word, held court.

Henry shook his head then took a slow deep breath. *I am being judgemental without true cause*, he thought. *I must afford him the benefit of the doubt before I make any snap judgements.* So he did; and by the time another three days had passed he had arrived at that judgement: "He's a total 'Triple Grade A' Arsehole," Henry muttered into his quiche and chips. Seconds later Max the Magnificent had looked across at him, smiled, turned back to his harem, grinned, then said something that caused them to giggle and glance across at him sitting alone; before returning their attention to their hero who had been telling them about his holiday home *pied-a-terre* in Marbella apparently.

"And how about you Henry?" Max said loudly.

"Pardon?"

"Winter holidays..."

"Pardon?"

"Where...Are...You...Going...For...Winter...Hols?" Max said slowly as though talking to a mentally challenged 98 year old (cue a gaggle of giggles). "Is it perhaps Blackpool for the winter lights?" (More giggles).

"Er...no... Actually, I am going to...er... Austria for the skiing..." The words had no sooner tripped off his traitorous tongue and out between his loose lips when he thought *Oh sugar, please don't let him be an Olympic standard downhill skier!* Max raised an eyebrow in surprise.

"Oh...right...When are you going then?"

"Two weeks..."

"Oh right; well you must bring us back some photo's, hey ladies?" The gaggle giggled as Henry thought *'Oh sugar, there goes my Blackpool break then...'*

***

The travel agent 'hmmmed' "You've left it a little late sir, but we'll do our best. Now let me see..." he said scrolling through his desktop computer. "Ah yes! We can do you a week in Mayrhofen in the Tyrol. It's a

5

pretty little village about an hour's drive from Innsbruck and it sits at the foot of the Ziller valley. And it has, let me see... it has 136 *piste* kilometres and 57 lifts... and the slopes rise to some 2,500 metres..."

"A hundred and thirty six *piste* kilometres and fifty seven lifts," Henry said coolly like an aficionado of winter sports.

"That's right sir and slopes rising to 2,500 metres."

"Two thousand five hundred metres. That's quite high then," Henry said slowly.

"Certainly is sir, perhaps not as high as you are probably used to, but high enough that one would not want to come down from it head first!"

"No, one would not," Henry said slowly as he reached into an inside pocket for his wallet and somewhat reluctantly took out a credit card.

***

The 'fasten seat belt' sign pinged on and Henry repeated for the umpteenth time in the last fortnight: "I'm sure it will be an adventure." And he had almost convinced himself that it would; until the travel agent's '2,500 metres' crept back again into his mind.

The little turbo-prop plane had about forty other passengers and he was quietly pleased to see that they were for the most part, couples of about his own age, as well as one or two with pre-teen children.

As he looked around his mind slid back to the last time he had sat in a plane. It was about ten years earlier when he had booked his only other holiday abroad. It was to Cyprus, where as an avid reader of all things ancient Greek and fostered by reading Greek classics and Myths from writers such as Robert Graves, he hoped to immerse himself in the culture.

Unfortunately, he had booked his holiday to a place called *Ayia Napa*.

He shuddered as images of loud drunken foul mouthed youths and equally loud drunken foul mouthed, mascara smeared, false eye-lashed and scantily clad girls, rampaged through his mind... stopping only to upchuck the contents of their stomachs in pretty Technicolor streams. He shuddered again and dragged himself back to the here and now. "It will be an adventure," he mouthed. And it would be; only he had no idea just how much of an adventure fate or rather, divine intervention, had in store for him...

The flight was quite smooth, until they encountered the Alps and turbulence bounced them about. He looked out of the window and muttered "Oh sugar!" as the needle sharp teeth below almost seemed to reach up in an effort to swallow plane and passengers.

He heaved a little sigh of relief as the wheels touched down and within half an hour he was, along with four other couples, aboard a silver minibus that purred along a well tarred road on a gradual upward route. *'Two thousand five hundred metres'*, he thought.

The drive was pleasant and the hour quickly passed.

"We arrive in Mayrhofen in five minutes," the driver announced. And true to his word they were soon driving down the busy little main street, passing couples and groups of promenading holidaymakers. The driver called out a Hotel name and pulled over as a couple rose from their seats. They followed him out of the bus to pick up their baggage and within a minute he was back inside and on to the next hotel.

Henry was the last passenger in the bus when the driver turned off the main street and pulled up at a three storey Tyrolean style building with its pitched roof and wooden window shutters, each of which had diamond shaped centre cut outs. Henry picked up his suitcase and thanked the driver before making his way up the hotel approach, through the front door and into the foyer area. There he walked over to the reception counter where an attractive early middle aged blond woman with twin thick plaits in her hair and wearing a pristine white blouse with a gold enamelled name tag that read 'Trudy' pinned just above her ample left breast, stood expectantly. She greeted him with a smile. "Mister Pratt?" she asked.

Henry returned the smile shyly and nodded.

"Your journey was pleasant?" she said in accented English. Henry nodded.

"Yes thank you, er, Trudy, except for some turbulence before we landed."

"Ah yes, it is the mountains. The winds can be much blowy," then: "And is it your first time to Mayrhofen Mr Pratt?"

"Yes, and in fact, it is my first time to Austria." She clapped her hands.

"So, we must look after you much good!" Then: "So where do you do skiing before; Italy or Germany?" Henry shook his head.

"No, I don't do...I mean I have never been skiing before..." She clapped her hands again.

"So you are ski virgin!"

"Er, well, I suppose you could say that," he said blushing lightly.

"You will enjoy," she said firmly.

"I hope so, but I am a little nervous..."

"Why nervous?"

"I have heard that many people break legs skiing..." She puffed up her cheeks and blew air out dismissively.

"Only clever people who think after one lesson only they are champion skier!"

"Then I must find a ski instructor who will make sure I do not run before I walk!" he said with forced humour. She frowned lightly at the odd words.

"Ah, I see," she added as his meaning registered and her frown was replaced by a grin. "It is the English wit yes." He returned the smile. "So a good instructor, you must have."

"Indeed, one who will be very patient, I think," he replied seriously.

"Then my son Karl is the man for you. He has been instructor for one year and offers special rate for hotel guests."

"Excellent," Henry said softly... and a trifle flatly.

"And very soon you lose your cherry, yes, as I think English sometime say!" Henry blushed again.

"Er, yes, I have sometimes heard it put thus colourfully..." She frowned lightly as she struggled with the words, then grinned.

"Ah yes! It is the famous English sense of humour, I think, very...droll...is that the word?"

"Er, yes, I suppose so," he said as she

turned to take a card key from a hook and in a businesslike manner said:

"Your key Mr Pratt. Room 302 on the third floor; there is elevator to the left and please leave with me your passport."

Up in his room Henry took in the dark Tyrolean style wooden furniture and the Alpen scenes that decorated the walls before unpacking his suitcase and stowing his clothes away carefully so as not to add any more creases to those the trip had already caused.

He lay down on the bed. "It will be an adventure," he said firmly.

An hour or so later he decided to take the evening air with a little walk along the main street before he had an early night. He passed the reception desk which has now empty and made his way outside where he glanced up at a dark blue blanket of sky where someone had scattered huge handfuls of sparkling diamonds. He took a deep breath of the crisp air and nodded, before making his way back onto the still busy street with its souvenir shops, cafes, hotels and bars. He walked the length of the street, then crossed over and made his way back.

"Yes, it will be an adventure..." he repeated as he approached his hotel, where a delicious cup of hot chocolate awaited him

Chapter 2

Being a habitual early riser, he made his way down to the dining room at 7.30, and saw he was the first guest; which suited him fine as he always felt a little self conscious when entering a busy room. He made his way over to a long white cloth covered table and helped himself to coffee from a percolator, muesli and milk and croissants with jam. It was a major departure from his usual breakfast of sausage egg and beans, but, he admitted to himself that the 'continental' nature made a pleasant change.

He had finished before other guests began to appear and after self consciously returning a couple of "Good mornings," he quickly left for the solitude of his room where he read up on the resort via a few colourful leaflets and brochures that promoted the area. His reading was then interrupted by the ringing of his bedside telephone. It was Trudy, who told him that her son Karl could find a spare hour around two o'clock that afternoon, if that was convenient. "Yes," he said, as long as he was not putting anybody to any trouble. She assured him that Karl was happy to help a guest who his mother had recommended. He thanked her and was about to hang up, when, as an afterthought he said, "Skiing equipment; where can I hire that?"

"Don't worry," Trudy replied. "I will take you to the right place at, say, one o'clock."

"I don't want to put you to any trouble..." he managed before she cut in with a mock exasperated sigh.

"Really Henry, you English...always brought up to be so, how is it...proper... yes so very *proper and correct!*" Henry smiled thinly down the telephone.

"Perhaps that used to be the English way at one time Trudy. But nowadays good manners are not so common."

"Ah yes, perhaps you speak of the young, is it so Henry?"

"Well, yes, I find that is so often the case." *(Ayia Napa raised its ugly head again)*.

"Ah but the young have always been, how you say... *outré*, yes?" He almost delivered a firm 'no'. He had been young once and he had never been *outré*; never deviated from what was deemed correct and proper...*outré* indeed! The 'no' died on his lips and he merely offered a meek 'yes' before she hung up. He put the phone down and then another thought intruded...it seemed 'Mr Pratt' had become 'Henry'.

He made his way down to reception at precisely two minutes to one. Trudy, who was wearing a short black tailored jacket and black slacks was stood behind the counter with a young dark haired woman who was obviously about to stand in for her superior. "Exactly on time Henry," A smiling Trudy said glancing at her watch.

"You are sure it is no trouble..." Trudy placed her hands on her hips, tilted her head slightly to one side and said: "Hen...reee!"

"Sorry..."

They made their way onto the busy main street and then into a shop with a window display of skiing gear. Inside Trudy greeted a young woman assistant and then pointed to Henry. "This is my friend Henry," she said. "He is from England and he is a ski virgin." Henry smiled weakly. Fifteen minutes later the ski virgin was kitted out in a dark blue bobble hat, a light blue ski jacket with matching over trousers and mittens, a pair of goggles and a pair of clunky size 8 (continental size 42) ski boots. "Perfect," Trudy said. Henry, looking at himself in a full length mirror, was not so sure.

"It's a bit on the bright side," he said slowly.

"It is Perfect," Trudy said firmly.

The clothes and boots were placed in a

large shopping bag and Trudy picked out a pair of shiny black skis together with matching black ski poles to finish off the ensemble.

Back in his room at the hotel Henry took the clothes out of the bag and put them, the goggles and ski boots on before clipping the skis onto the boots and clunking his way over to the mirror. There he struck a professional downhill racing pose. "I still think it's a bit on the bright side," he muttered. But having said that, he did look rather dashing...

***

Kitted out and carrying his skis and poles, Henry made his way down to reception, where he found Trudy stood in conversation with a young fair haired slim and tallish man, who he presumed to be Karl. He was pleased to see that the man had an eminently sensible haircut...not a poncy pony tail.

Trudy introduced them and after a brief conversation Henry was also pleased to note that Karl seemed to be a very pleasant and grounded individual who did not carry so much as a trace of the increasingly common, 'dog's bollocks' gene.

Trudy reached up and planted a kiss on

Karl's cheek. "Now you must look after Henry," she said firmly. "He must come back with no broken bones!" Karl grinned, Henry smiled (very thinly).

Outside, they made their way down the main street before turning off and approaching a ski lift ticket booth that stood in front of a large cable car suspended on what Henry fervently hoped were very strong cables. The words *Two Thousand Five Hundred Metres* played quickly across his mind.

Karl showed the ticket master his professional instructor's season pass and Henry then bought a weekly pass that entitled him to use any of the resort's 57 lifts. They took their seats in the large gondola that was almost full of skiers and within two minutes they were off and climbing. Henry swallowed hard.

"This car is called the *Ahornbahn* and it is the biggest cable car in Austria. It takes us to *Leisure Mountain Ahorn* in about eight minutes," Karl said.

"Eight minutes climb, to the top of a mountain er, that's quite quick..."

"Yes, so not long before you will hit the *piste* Henry!"

"Er Excellent..."

The cable car came to a halt on a bright sun drenched plateau, the crisp white snow of which was dotted with dozens of darker shapes standing or whizzing about. The passengers climbed out and dispersed, with Karl leading Henry to a relatively flat roped off area. "This is the nursery slope Henry. We will start here for the basics." Henry nodded. It looked an innocent enough place where bones were not very likely to snap and splinter.

Karl spent a good few minutes explaining the basics of balance and weight distribution before going on to show Henry how to turn and stop safely. "Okay Henry," he then said. "So now you know how it is done in theory..." Henry swallowed.

"Er, it looks a little bit steep here, can we find somewhere a little flatter?"

"No, Henry, any flatter and you will be simply stood still..." That didn't sound like a bad idea to Henry; but he took a deep breath and thought: *It will be an adventure.*

"Right," he said firmly, "Let's do it."

"Okay Henry, I am just behind you, line your skis up straight and as far apart as we said. Good, that's perfect. Now plant the poles, bend your knees slightly and PUSH."

"Oh sugar!" Henry muttered as he began to inch forward.

"Good Henry!" Karl said from behind. "Good, now a little bit more push with the poles...Good now you are moving...nicely!"

Henry's heart began to race as his

speed suddenly picked up until he was careering along at a giddying five miles per hour!

"Excellent Henry! You look like a natural!" The words of encouragement registered and he suddenly realised that yes, he was doing quite well!

He dug his poles in a little harder and his speed shot up to at least 10 miles per hour! Actually, this was fun!

And there and then on an Austrian ski slope, a little spark of elation ignited in his breast.

He had never excelled at anything remotely sports related in his life and now, here he was being told that he was a natural at skiing!

His hour came to an end too soon and on the way back down to Mayrhofen Henry asked Karl when he could fit him in for another lesson. Karl said he had a slot available at 11 in the morning if that was convenient. "Great!" said Henry; "But can we go on a quicker slope?"

Over the next four days Henry had four one hour lessons, at the end of which Karl shook his head after being asked for another the next day. "No Henry," Karl said firmly. "I am booked solid for the next week; and anyway, I would just be taking your money for the sake of it. You have done all the beginners' slopes and there is nothing more I can show you... it is time for you to go solo."

Back in his hotel room Henry, still on a high, reached for one of the brochures he had browsed through on his second day. "Yes," he said to himself, "This was the one." The brochure had the title *Action Mountain Penken* and below a picture of a snow clad peak were the bold words: ***Harakiri: The Perfect Thrill***. He scanned through the brochure until he found what he was looking for. He read: *Now just a few minutes from the bustling centre of Mayrhofen you will find the coolest challenge in winter sports: the famous Harakiri, Austria's steepest slope adventure at 78%. Anyone who handles this descent gets to wear the 'I Survived Harakiri' T- shirt and qualify for a free photo shoot on a Friday from 1pm to 3pm.* "A free photo," he mused. "Now that would take a bit of wind out of the sails of a certain pony tailed cretin..."

Chapter 3

That night he dreamed he was, for once, the centre of attention. And in his dream he revelled in it! Flashbulbs popped and a throng of shouting reporters vied for his attention. He raised his hands and with a 'whoa, calm down chaps' gesture assured them that they could all have a piece of him, but they would have to form an orderly queue...

He woke refreshed; and more than that, he woke with an odd and strangely alien feeling that he couldn't at first put his finger on. And then it hit him...it was Confidence (With a capital C!).

He sang in the shower and hummed to himself as he shaved and dressed. He skipped down the stairs rather than taking the lift and when fellow guests entered the dining room he beat them to a cheery "Good morning."

On his way out of the dining room he almost bumped into Trudy. "Oops Sorry!" he said with a smile as they nearly collided face to face. Trudy, startled more by his sunny attitude than the near miss, returned the smile.

"My word Henry, losing your cherry

seems to have put you in a good mood!"

"I lost that when I was twenty-five!" he said. Trudy frowned lightly but then, as she caught his meaning:

"Oh...I do not think we speak of the same cherry you naughty man!" The Old Henry would certainly have blushed at this juncture, but the apparently New Henry did not; his grin merely widened.

Four hours later he stood on the bottom loading station of the recently launched *3S Penkenbahn*, a 33 gondola cable car network at the base of *Action Mountain Penken* that took passengers to the *Vans Penken Park*, rated one of the best snow parks in Europe.

As he waited in a small queue of skiers and snow boarders for a gondola to arrive at the docking station, he again marvelled at the remarkable change in attitude that had come about due to Karl's words of praise...and the fact that he had actually ended up enjoying his first and only success (minor, or not) at anything remotely sports related.

He was still lost in admiration for his remarkable prowess, when the gondola slid into place, disgorged its passengers and dragged his mind back to the here and now.

The ascent took less than 10 minutes and soon he was clipping on his skis on one of the intermediate *pistes* that catered for skiers with some experience. "This mountain doesn't look that imposing," he said to himself as he took in the surrounding snow clad and cloud covered peaks that towered over *Penken.*

After an hour on the *piste* he reckoned he was warmed up enough to take on this so called beast, *The Harakiri.* "I can't wait to see their faces when I show them the photo," he said with the trace of a smirk on his face.

***

"Oh Sugar!" he gasped ten minutes later when he stood on the edge of what appeared to be an almost perpendicular drop. He glanced around desperately to see if anyone was looking. There was nobody behind him. He dug his poles in and made a move to edge backward. Unfortunately it was only the pole tips that moved backwards while his body was propelled forwards...over the edge...

"ARRRGGGHH!" He yelled and then: "OOOHSUUGGGAAARRR!" As the ground fell away and his skis slapped down onto hard 78% angled snow.

"FEETTOGETHER!" He screamed as visions of multiple snapped bones flashed across his mind. "DONTPANIC!" He ordered his brain as within seconds he was hurtling downwards at a speed that to him seemed to be somewhere around *Mach III.*

Thirty seconds that were more like three hours to him dragged by and...He hadn't fallen! He was still in one piece! "You can do this!" he screamed against the wind that was threatening to tear his goggles and nose off his face. "You can d...WHAT THE FUU!..." He managed as from nowhere a huge spruce tree sprang into existence right in front of him... SMMAACKKK...

The world froze around him, there was then a brief 'moment' of darkness, before he suddenly began to rise slowly up THROUGH the snow covered branches of the tree!

He gasped, and looked down...to see his crumpled body lying on its back with a slowly spreading halo of crimson staining the snow around his head. "Oh sugar," he murmured. "It looks like I'm dead..."

Chapter 4

He took a deep breath, then thought: *That's odd, if I'm dead, how come I can still breathe? And if I am really dead where the heck am I going now?*

He continued to rise right up through the tree and as he broke through the foliage cover into bright sunlight he began to drift towards an escalator. He blinked and rubbed his eyes. Yes, it was an actual escalator IN THE SKY. And that was not all, there were a number of other people dressed in white smocks on the escalator and...He glanced down at his own torso; he was dressed the same way! *Odder and Odder*, he thought as without any conscious effort on his own part he drifted over to and then on to the bottom rising stair.

Above him the head of the escalator broke through low cloud and one by one the people in front began to step off. "Oh sugar!" he muttered, "It's a bloody long way down!" But then he thought *So what, the fall isn't going to kill me is it...* His turn came and he stepped off onto a yellow brick road that led to a huge pair of pearly gates...that were shut and had a note pinned to them that read *Closed for re-gilding, please make your way to the appropriately lettered turnstile.* There was also an arrow that pointed towards a huge circular stadium-like building some hundred yards away.

He slipped into a line of new arrivals heading towards the building and as he reached it he spotted that the first turnstile he came to had a huge letter 'N' above it, while underneath this there was a large monitor screen with slowly scrolling red neon script.

He saw 'Newspapers': (Owners) (Editors), (Reporters), and then watched until they were repeated, before moving on to the letter 'O'. This letter showed 'Occasional Saints', One Time Presidents and Premiers.' He watched until they scrolled round again, before moving on to turnstile 'P', where he pulled up sharply. 'P' was showing 'Politicians' (General), 'Politicians' (Would be), 'Powder' (Soap), 'Powder' (Puff) Manufacturers.

"Powder, brackets, Soap Manufacturers!" he exclaimed. "That's me!" He moved up to the turnstile and someone behind bumped into him "What the..." he said before turning around to see a rather Effeminate looking chubby and balding man stood with one hand on a hip.

"Hello ducky," the man lisped. Henry turned from the man to the sign, then back again. "Er... politician are you?"

"No dear...Powder Manufacturer..."

"Soap?"

"No dear, Puff."

"Figgers." Said Henry as he moved forward a little nervously; just before a voice from inside the turnstile demanded: "NEXT!"

Henry stepped forward.

"Name," said a bored looking, middle aged round faced and rather plump man who was sat on a stool behind a grill. Henry blinked. The man had a halo hovering over his head! Henry also noticed that he was dressed in a grubby off white robe.

"Er, excuse me sir," Henry said. "I am a little confused... can you tell me where I am?"

"You're at turnstile 'P'."

"No, I mean where am I actually?" The man sighed lightly.

"You are," he said, before breaking into song, "Everywhere and nowhere baby, that's where you're at..."

"Pardon?"

"That's a line from an old pop song; bit before your time probably. So let me put it another way in song: You're knock, knock, knocking on Heaven's door..."

"Oh, right!"

"Okay, now we've sorted that out, name please." Henry was about to answer when a thought struck him.

"Can I just ask you one more question please?" The operator sighed again.

"If you must..."

"Well, I was in Austria before my...accident. And I joined a lot other people on an escalator and then a big crowd of other people making their way to this stadium thing..."

"And?" the operator said in a bored voice.

"Well it has just struck me that on the way to this turnstile I caught quite a few snatches of conversation...and they were all in English...Why is that when I was in Austria and all, or most of the people who were on that escalator should probably have been speaking Austrian... they were not?"

"It's down to the Big Man. He reckons we need a lingua...lingua...What's that Latin name I'm looking for?"

"Lingua franca?"

"That's it! Like you see with pilots and air traffic controllers; makes for less confusion."

"Oh, right. So if say, a Borneo head hunter arrived he would automatically speak English...if he had a head of course?" The operator sighed again.

"Correct squire, he would have a head and automatically speak English, The *lingua franca*; although probably with a Borneo accent." Henry, who was blessed, or cursed, with an inquisitive mind, was on the verge of asking what a Borneo accent would sound like; but a quick glance at the operator's face stopped him. Instead he said "Thank you, please carry on."

"Right, as I was saying before twenty questions: NAME?"

"Er, Henry Pratt, with two tees."

"Occupation prior to demise?"

"Powder brackets Soap, Manufacture; although strictly speaking I was on the research and development side..." Big Sigh.

"Powder brackets Soap will suffice. So now we're got that sorted," he said moving his hand towards a red button at his side "Seeing as you're one of that lot, send you down shall we... to Old Nick right away should we?"

"Old Nick!" Henry said. "What, you mean... THE Old Nick!"

"Yeah. Save time shall we," the man repeated as his hand lowered towards the button.

"NO! Wait a minute!" Henry yelled, as a trembling in his legs transmitted itself to the floor that seemed also to tremble. He glanced down and suddenly realised he was standing on a trap door! The man shrugged.

"Oh, okay, if you insist...but always go

the same way your lot... along with most of them politicians."

"No! I mean...I'm not a bad person... I'm honest...honest!" The man slid open a draw and removed a card.

"Right then, let's see...Powder Manufacturer, brackets, Soap... Right...Have you ever put the word 'New' on a product just to con the customer?"

"No, never!" The man glanced to his right at a dial that had the word 'truth' on one side and 'lie' on the other, with a needle in the middle. The needle swung to 'truth'.

"Okay. How about the word 'Improved?'"

"No..." The needle swung to 'truth'.

"Okay. Did you ever use actresses posing as housewives in supermarkets...and offered to give them two for one?"

"Certainly not!" The needle swung to 'truth'.

"Hmmm. How about cute little puppies?"

"Nope." 'truth.'

"Bikini clad dolly birds?

"Nope." 'truth.'

"My word! What's the name of this powder of yours, Zad? Ono? Turf?"

"No."

"Hairy Snow? New Improved Mold Fourteen?

"No. Give up?"

"Okay...I give up...what?"

"Soap Powder."

"Soap Powder!"

"Yep."

"Well, can't say I've ever heard of that one!"

"Ah well not surprising really, it's a brand ne..."

"AHA!" the man said reaching for the red button.

"NO! I wasn't going to say the 'new', word! It's *'never'* been marketed before. That's what I was about to say..."

"You sure?"

"Yes!" The needle swung to 'truth'.

"And this 'Soap Powder', good is it?"

"Yes, and if you don't mind me saying..."

"What?"

"Well, no offence, but I couldn't help noticing..."

"What?"

"I mean, your attire, not too sparkling white is it...man in your position...front line troop so to speak..." The man glanced down at his robe.

"Yeah well, it's all that ambrosia like..."

"What, you mean rice pudding?"

"No the food of the Gods Ambrosia...

that an' the Manna...perfect for moppin' up the gravy is Manna...Anyway squire, looks like you passed the test." He then, reached into a drawer and removed a shiny new halo, which he passed through the grill to Henry. "Just plonk it over your head squire and it will stay there." He then leaned forward and pressed the button that released the lock on the turnstile.

"Thanks," Henry said turning his eyes up and catching a glimpse of the golden ring.

"No probs. Maybe we can meet up later for a pint if you want and I can help fill you in on the gaff?"

"That would be most pleasant..."

"Okay, I'm off duty shortly, so see you down *The Angel* around nine o'clock. It's not hard to find...it's on *Apostle's Avenue*. Just ask anyone for directions."

Henry thanked him and had just passed through the turnstile, when his new acquaintance, who was on the verge of shouting "NEXT"suddenly sat bolt upright.

"Wait a minute, Henry Pratt!" He turned to a laptop computer behind him. "E-Mail, I'm sure there was an E-Mail about a Henry Pratt..." He brought the inbox up and yes...there it was. 'A1 Priority: Henry Pratt: Report arrival immediately to code 777.'

"Code Seven, Seven, Seven, that's a hotline straight through to... Bloody He...!"

He turned his eyes upwards and with hands clasped said "Sorry." He then reached for a telephone by his side and nervously keyed in three digits. There was a click as the line came alive and he could hear background noises that sounded oddly like moaning and cracking of whips. He frowned lightly before a voice shouted "HELLO!"

"Er, hello...can you put me through to the Boss please..."

"Nah, he's not here...nipped down to earth again...gone to stir up some more shit in the Middle East..."

"Er, what number is this?"

"Six, Six, Six."

"Bloody He..." He quickly turned his eyes up and whispered "Sorry..."

"Sorry fer what?"

"Er, sorry...wrong number..." He placed the handset down gingerly, before picking it up again and carefully dialling 777. The line came alive and a woman's voice said "Head Office, how may I help you?"

"Er, can you put me through to the Boss please..."

"He's... very busy, is your call urgent?"

"Very. It concerns a red flag memo on a Henry Pratt..."

"Hold the line please, and I think I can connect you to his Son..." Celestial harp music played for a minute before...

"Hello?" Henry took a deep breath.

"Hello Sir, Powder, brackets, Soap Powder, brackets Puff Manufacturers, here Sir...He's arrived!" He listened intently, interjecting the odd respectful "Yes sir." Then: "Yes Sir! Right away Sir! You can count on me Sir!" He placed the phone down reverently and mouthed "Bloody Hell!" Before springing to his feet, placing a 'Closed' sign over the grill and exiting 'toot sweet'.

***

Jesus put the phone down and frowned lightly. *Not really My business*, He thought. *But until Dad gets his act together, I suppose I have to get involved*. He nodded to Himself, then picked up the phone again and pressed the intercom button. "Joan, can you come through please." Seconds later there was a light tap on his office door and Joan of Arc entered.

"Yes Sir?"

"Has He had his medication today?"

"No Sir, but He is due shortly." Jesus sighed.

"And the plagues; are they still occurring?"

"Unfortunately they are Sir. Yesterday it was frogs. The cleaning department had the de...a heck of a job rounding up and catching all the little buggers..." Jesus sighed again.

"So, we've had frogs and lice; that leaves flies and locusts. Well let's hope the medication can help to snap Him out of His Old Testament mood sooner rather than later...*apropos* of which; when is His next golf match with Lucifer due?"

"Just a moment Sir and I will go and check." Joan left the office and then returned two minutes later. "On Thursday Sir." Jesus sighed again and shook His head.

"So we could have to put up with more bloody plagues of insects before then...the cleansing department will be well pissed off. Only good thing I suppose is that while He's secured in his quarters the infestation is only local and we won't have the other bloody plagues loosed throughout Heaven. That would be bad news for sure and particularly so if He got it into His head to do the whole ten plagues not just the insects and frogs. Imagine if we had to deal with 'Water into Blood', 'Diseased Livestock', ' Boils', 'Thunderstorms, Hail and Fire', 'Darkness for Three Days' and 'Death of First Born!" Jesus then pursed His lips in thought.

"No, wait a minute, at least we can scrub that last one off, seeing as there can't be any 'first', second, third, or any other 'born', born up here; because that would be against the entry rules. Still," He continued, "the rest would be bad enough, with everyone wondering what the h...heck was going on.

"Anyway, no point in worrying too much about it just now. It's nearly lunch time, what do you fancy from the takeaway?" Joan shrugged lightly.

"Anything really Sir...except what You ordered last week if that's okay with You..."

"Last week? Why, what did I get you last week then?"

"A flame grilled steak Sir..."

"Oh, yeah, oops, sorry about that Joan..."

"That's okay Sir; it was a long time ago. But the memory of that fire still lingers..."

Chapter 5

Henry walked through a large and pretty park that contained a number of softly burbling marble fountains and a huge variety of gaily coloured flower beds. There were also dozens of trees with blushing cherry pink or pristine apple white blossoms, where roosting Birds of Paradise added their own glorious colours to heavenly nature's gorgeous palette.

He passed rustic benches, some of which were occupied by other white gowned and halo wearing people; most of whom were engrossed in reading from what looked to be bibles. "I suppose I'll need to get one of those," he muttered. "Seeing as how it must be the *de rigueur* reading matter around here..."

He arrived at the edge of the park to see a white wooden signpost, much like an Estate Agents' board that had an arrow pointing to the right with red lettering underneath that said 'New Arrivals'. He turned right and exited the park through an open wrought iron gate that led to a broad thoroughfare lined with a multitude of what looked like multi storey apartments. He shrugged lightly. "Well I suppose the dead have to have somewhere to live," he muttered. And saying it, he stopped as a thought occurred to him. *Why did the dead have to have somewhere to live anyway?' Surely all they did was swan around all day twanging on little harps, didn't they? And what about sleeping and eating and drinking and...and...intimate relations between the sexes! Did all that actually happen here too? Well, yes, eating and drinking must do, because didn't his new friend, the turnstile keeper mention something about Ambrosia and Manna and gravy? And of course, he had an invitation to meet up with the turnstile keeper for a drink at a pub at nine o'clock!*

He shook his head in an effort to re-align a few billion brain cells which probably got scrambled by the sudden and intimate contact with that bloody tree. It didn't work. He shook his head again and carried on walking until he saw another signboard at a junction. This one was identical to the one in the park, except the arrow pointed left and the red lettering said *'New Arrivals Three Hundred Meters'.*

"Bloody metric! Bloody American spelling!" He muttered; before thinking: *I seem to be using a lot of coarse language lately. I wonder if that is going to get me in trouble with the Management?*

Three hundred *Metres* later he stood in front of an impressive looking glass fronted building that announced itself in brash five foot high bold italicised chrome letters as *'New Arrivals'*.

"Another sop to the 'in your face' attitude of our Trans-Atlantic cousins," he said adding a sigh of resignation as he mounted the steps and negotiated his way through a revolving door and over to the closest of at least a dozen queues lined up in front of desks manned by white gowned receptionists. He glanced towards the elderly white bearded man who sat behind the desk in his queue. For a second he thought it might be HIM; but he immediately rejected that thought. HE was the Big Boss and HE was surely above manning a common reception desk! He checked the other desks. They all seemed to be manned by much younger men.

The Reception to Heaven! he thought, *Of course, the Pearly Gates! They were closed for re-gilding. And who was it that, tradition had it, met New Arrivals at those Pearly Gates and logged them in through The Book of Life? Saint Peter, that's who!' I must be in the queue that the leading apostle heads up!*

Henry approached the desk slowly as the queue in front of him gradually dwindled down and arrivals were dealt with before each of them left carrying a single sheet of paper.

He reached the desk and as the old man looked up from his Apple Mac computer to ask his name, Henry said "It's you isn't it!" The target of his statement narrowed his eyes.

"What?"

"It is you isn't it!" Henry said. The old man sighed.

"Last time I looked in the mirror, yes, it was me."

"Saint Peter!"

"Right, now we have that sorted... NAME?" Henry detected the note of annoyance and decided it would be in his best interest to get everything onto a businesslike footing.

"Henry Pratt, with two tees" he said formally. Saint Peter typed the name into his computer then pressed the 'enter' key. The machine spat a raspberry back at him.

"Buggarit!" Saint Peter said. Henry leaned forward to look at the monitor.

"Er, you've spelt it wrong..."

"What?"

"You've spelt Henry 'H.E.N.T.R.Y.'"

"Hentry?"

"Yes." Saint Peter peered closely at the monitor screen.

"Bloody fingers like sausages... must have pressed the R and T at the same time."

"Easy mistake to make, I suppose."

"Bloody computers! Never had this trouble with the old fashioned but very reliable *Book of Life!*"

"Why did you change then?" Saint Peter sniffed.

"Head Office. The Boss' Son got it into His head."

"What? JC Himself!"

"Yes, He's turned into a Moderniser lately."

"And you're not into technology then?"

"I'm Old School, and bloody proud of it!" Henry tried a bit of light hearted levity.

"Maybe He still had it in for you and decided to get His own back..." Saint Peter's eyes narrowed.

"In for me? Why would He have it in for me?"

"You know; back in that garden with the cock crowing thrice and you like saying, you didn't know Him..." Saint Peter's mouth hardened.

"I was only human then. And He does not bear grudges."

"Oh right. So, any way, you would still like to do things the old way, like you did them before?" Saint Peter nodded firmly.

"Now it's all bloody emails and floppy dicks and such..."

"Discs..."

"What?"

"You said floppy dicks. It's floppy *discs*."

"Dicks...Discs...What's the difference!"

"Quite a lot actually... And any way floppies have been replaced ages ago by compact *discs*." Saint Peter shrugged as he retyped the name and pressed 'enter'. This time he was rewarded with a snatch of pleasant harp music. "Right," he said. "You are logged in at 14.30 hours...Half past two in the afternoon," he added firmly for tradition's sake. He then pressed another key and a printer spat out a sheet of paper, which he handed to Henry. "Directions to your death quarters and some information on 'do's and 'don'ts'", he said.

"Er, how do I get in when I get there then?" Saint Peter sighed.

"The best way is through the front door I would have thought..."

"Then I need a key." Saint Peter sighed again and turned his eyes upward.

"It's Heaven," he said slowly, "Not bloody Hell... No locks...NEXT!"

***

Henry glanced around the light and airy snug of *The Angel* and noted that the clientele seemed to well match the pub's name. There were a number of black suited white collared priests/vicars, brown or grey habit clad monks, four nuns and two Salvationists (carrying red collection boxes), as well as a few white gown clad laity.

"Ah, there he is..." he said as he spotted the turnstile keeper stood at the bar chatting to a rather pretty barmaid. Henry made his way over to the man's side, cleared his throat, tapped lightly on the man's shoulder and said "Er, hello." The turnstile keeper turned around.

"Oh good, you made it then... Henry...you don't mind if I call you Henry do you?"

"No, of course not er..."

"Herbert, Herbert Postlethwaite." Henry nodded.

"Fine old northern surname that. Don't know where my surname, Pratt, comes from though..."

"Could be anywhere really...seein' as how the world is full of Pratts..." Henry frowned lightly.

"Full? Hardly, it's not as though it was Smith, or Jones."

"It was a joke Henry; you know like how people call other people who they are not particularly fond of...Pratts..."

"Oh, right...very droll..." Herbert rolled his eyes.

"Anyway Henry, I'm in the chair; what'll you have?" Henry was about to say that Herbert was in fact standing; so how could he be 'in the chair'; but he decided that one little joke was enough for the day.

"Thank you Herbert, I'll have a lager please."

"Two bottles of lager, sweetheart," Herbert said to the barmaid, who smiled, turned round to a cooler cabinet opened the door, then bent down to remove two bottles of *Harp* lager... in the act of which her mini-robe rode up her thighs. Henry and Herbert's eyes automatically locked on; while the halo's above their heads began to slowly rise.

Oh my, Henry thought, *we may be dead, but some things never change*! He glanced at Herbert, who nodded. "Just think of jumping into an ice cold shower..." He said matter-of-factly; and by the time the barmaid had turned around, placed the lagers on the bar, twisted off the caps then placed glasses next to them, their rogue halos had subsided.

"Enjoy gentlemen," she said in a sexy voice that sounded to Henry like someone slowly pouring a bottle of Guinness into a glass half full of brown sugar.

Henry reached for his bottle and began to pour into his glass, when the barmaid said "I haven't seen you before Henry, new are you?" Henry took a sip of the ice cold beer.

"Er, yes I am, in fact this is my first day...and you, how long have you been here?"

"Not long; about eighty-five years, I think."

"Not long... only eighty-five years...five minutes really..." Herbert butted in.

"Sorry to interrupt squire, but there is something *very* important we need to discuss. Grab your beer and let's find a quiet corner." Curious, Henry followed Herbert to an empty table.

"Nice in here isn't it?" Henry said glancing around the pub.

"What? Oh yeah, it gets a bit boring though sometimes."

"Boring? What do you mean boring?"

"You know same old, same old..." He pointed over to where two nuns were playing darts with little golden bows and arrows next to two clergymen involved in a riveting game of Ludo.

"Same old menu," Herbert said pointing to a menu board on the bar wall that showed: 'Adam's Ale, Devilled Kidneys and Angel Delight'.

"Same boring trips," he continued pointing out another poster that advertised 'All Heaven Snakes and Ladders Competition', 'Inter-Sector Flower Arranging Knock-Out Competition' and a 'Cloud

Spotting Week-end'.

"Same crappy music," he sighed as he pointed to one corner where a little ancient pianist, wearing an expression of near terminal boredom, was tinkling out '*Mares eat oats and does eat oats and little lambs eat ivy.*' Henry nodded.

"I see what you mean; but the music's not *too* bad. He does hit a few right notes ...here and there..."

"Yeah, suppose so. And every now and again he changes the tune to 'Three Steps to Heaven'. And sometimes he gets really edgy by murderin' 'That Old Devil Moon'. ANYWAY, never mind the music. Like I said, we have something very important to discuss."

"Yes?"

"You are/were someone who knows/knew about soap powders, right?"

"Well yes, I do/did have a certain reputation in that particular area..."

"You do/did?"

"Yes I dood, I mean did."

"Right, well listen...We are being infiltrated!"

"Infiltrated!"

"Shhh!"

"Sorry...What do you mean Infiltrated?" Henry whispered.

"HELL."

"No need to snap, I only asked..."

"No...Hell, Hell is infiltrating us."

"Hell is infiltrating us?"

"Shhh!"

"Sorry."

"Just listen. Some time ago The Boss negotiated an agreement with Lucy..."

"Lucy?"

"Lucifer. The Boss calls him Lucy, just to wind him up..."

"Oh, right. What kind of agreement?"

"An agreement beneficial to both parties."

"About what?"

"There are a lot of smokers up here, right?"

"Well yes, I suppose there might be."

"And what do smokers need to light up their fags and pipes...matches, right?"

"Right."

"And who do you think has cornered the market in that inflammable stuff, phosphorus, that's used for matches?"

"Right! Lucy, I mean Lucifer!"

"Shhh!"

"Sorry."

"Right, so The Boss, who incidentally is quite partial to the odd pipe of *Saint Bruno,* negotiated an agreement whereby they supply us with matches for a consideration."

"Which is?"

"Their head honchos get to come up here on holiday now and again to enjoy the odd change of scenery and climate."

"Aren't we worried about the corrupting influence?"

"Nah, they're pretty corrupt by the time they get here...Oh, I see what you mean. No they are kept under supervision. Plus they're restricted to the sector set aside for Used Car Salesmen; plenty of room there, for some reason or other."

"Right, so what's the problem?"

"Well the Boss, he knows Lucy, or Old Nick, or Satan whatever, from way back. Doesn't trust him one little bit. So He arranged for an undercover agent to slip down there," Herbert pointed downwards with his thumb, "and do a bit of snooping."

"Makes sense."

"Yeah; but it looks like our agent has been rumbled, as after he filed a report that indicates that there is indeed some Devilment underfoot, the hidden tracker he was wearing has not moved for a couple of months." Henry nodded slowly then he frowned.

"Look, this is all very interesting and all that; but what has it got to do with me?"

"You're an authority on soap powder..."

"And?"

"AND all your lot are down there. AND in his last report our agent said they were having lots of problems with their laundry and none of their experts could sort it out. AND Old Nick is a snappy dresser AND he's been making death hell for everyone down there, 'cause of this laundry problem." Henry shrugged.

"Well, he would be wouldn't he; it sort of comes with the territory doesn't it?"

"Well yeah, but the situation provides the Boss with a reason to offer a helping hand by sending down someone, who just happens to be *the* leading expert in the laundry business who could snoop around while he was tackling the problem!"

"Oh, right. So all we need now is some idiot who will risk discovery and subsequently be forced to spend the rest of eternity stoking bloody great fires!"

"Well... Yeah..."

"FORGET IT!"

"Shhh!"

"Sorry; but forget it! I've only been here five minutes and you expect me to risk everything..." Herbert shook his head slowly.

"Not me sunshine."

"Who then?" Herbert clasped his hands together in a praying pose and nodded slowly in a knowing way.

"What? You mean HIM?"

"Himself personally. Get Me Henry Pratt," He said. "Only man for the job," He said. Henry blinked.

"My word! When did HE say that then?"

"Today."

"Today?" Henry frowned lightly.

"Wait a minute. This morning I was skiing down a mountain and this bloody great tree appeared out of nowhere and..."

"Ahem...yes...well..."

"It did appear out of nowhere...that bloody great tree. SMACK!"

"Shhh!"

"Don't you shush me! It was planned wasn't it!"

"Okay, okay. But look, you were due soon anyway."

"Soon, how soon?"

"Thirty seven years... more or less."

"Thirty seven years, more or less. Oh that's alright then! So it didn't make much difference did it! I mean what would I have done with my life in another thirty seven years eh?"

"Well, to be honest, if your computer file is anything to go by...not a lot..."

"I could have been a late bloomer."

"Yeah, and hell might freeze over tomorrow..." Henry was a man not given to flights of fancy, so he nodded slowly.

"Okay, so I probably wouldn't have done much; but even so it would have been nice to have found out."

"Yeah I can see that; but hey, look at it this way; yes you were hustled...a bit," Henry pulled a wry face. "But the Boss needed you. Don't you think that makes you special? Over seven billion people down there on earth and who does He send for? Does He send for the Ghostbusters? No! He sends for the only man who He can rely on... Henry Pratt that's who!"

"Well I suppose, if you put it that way," Henry said.

Chapter 6

"Right," Henry said. "So let's go through the plan again.

"After a briefing from Head Office security we take the connecting lift to Purgatory, where we pretend we are doing a spot check to make sure nobody is getting out before their time is up. Then while I'm supposedly checking the books, you contact our man on site and arrange for him to take us down in the hidden lift to the Other Place."

"Correct."

"Then once we get down there our papers provided by security will give us the freedom to nose around under cover of trying to get to the bottom of the laundry problem."

"Correct."

"Also, while we are nosing around we will hopefully discover what happened to our missing agent and with a bit of luck rescue him..."

"Correct."

"Well, there you are then...piece of bloody cake!"

"Do I detect a note of sarcasm there squire?"

"You certainly do, *squire* and..." Henry was about to add something else, when a thought struck him "Anyway, I just realised I've been using the pronoun 'we' during this conversation; why *are* you coming with me on this mad escapade?"

"Ah, well, ahem, I need the brownie points."

"Why?"

"Well I sometimes do a little black market trading between regions and I got a tip off that it might have been noted by the wrong people; so a suicide mission can only do me good."

"SUICIDE MISSION!"

"Shhh!

"Sorry. What do you mean suicide mission!"

"Just a figure of speech squire. You won't have found out yet but the dead down below might top themselves or be killed again; and yes, they can experience real pain that hurts like...well like Hell. But permanent death after death is not on the cards."

"Oh, right, that makes me feel *so* much better. I can suffer hideous torture; like being roasted on a spit; but then I will recover, so that I can be roasted again and again, right?"

"Er, yeah, in theory."

"Oh jolly dee for me!" Henry said sarcastically before taking a deep breath and getting back down to the business in hand. "And anyway, where is this Security Chief who is supposed to meet us here for a briefing?"

"'Nosy' Parker, you mean? He's here somewhere," Herbert said softly as he scanned the room, before doing a quick double take and stopping on a man wearing sun glasses, a false beard and a turned up collar on his robe who was sat with a plastic shopping bag on his lap. "And I think I might have just spotted him..."

The man got to his feet and began to casually stroll over in their direction. "He's coming," Henry whispered. "Play it cool... And so," he said in a louder voice, "I said to Princess Anne try a shorter rein..." The man stopped directly in front of their table and spoke out of the side of his mouth.

"You Pratt?" He said to Henry.

"Charming! I mean I didn't come here to be insu..."

"Name Pratt, not Nature."

"Oh, I see...yes that's me, and are you..."

"Mary had a little lamb, its fleece was black as charcoal..." Henry frowned.

"Pardon?" Herbert stepped in.

"It's the coded introduction," he whispered to Henry. "I'll give him the reply. "Ahem: and every time it jumped the fence it scratched its little arsehole..."

"Response correct," Parker said.
Herbert nodded.

"Say no more squire, care to join us?"
Parker looked quickly left and right, then
moving forward he bumped into a chair that
Herbert had nudged out from the table.

"Damn cheap glasses!" the security
chief said.

"Tell you what squire," Herbert
offered, "While we're down there we will see
if we can pick you up a pair of Ray Bans.
Bound to have some decent ones, what with
the glare from the fires and things..." Parker
looked over the top of his glasses at Herbert
and frowned.

"Postlethwaite, isn't it?" Herbert
nodded. Parker raised an eyebrow.

"Oh yes, you're on file boy...bit of a
mister-fix-it eh?"

"Me squire! No not really...Do the odd
little favour now and then...just to help my
celestial brothers and sisters like..."

"What, like the carton of Ambrosia ice
lollies that somehow found their way to
Hades in exchange for a 20 pound tin of
vindaloo curry; that sort of help?" Herbert
opened his mouth, on the verge of protesting
his innocence, but Parker held a hand up and
tapped the side of his nose with the forefinger
of his other hand.

"Say no more boy. It's been noted...all noted." Henry, who had been sat quietly during the conversation, cleared his throat loudly.

"Excuse me Mr Parker," he said. "I'm the one the Boss sent for personally...*Before Time...*" He glanced across sourly at Herbert. "Can we please get on with this briefing now?"

Ten minutes later after a crash course in counter intelligence methods and surveillance techniques, the head of security stood up and beckoned them to follow him.

"Whoa," Henry said. "Right, I think we've got it now, but before we go any further, don't you think we'll like, be a little bit obvious, strolling around the underworld with these hanging above our heads," he pointed to his halo.

"Taken care of Pratt," the security chief said as he delved into the bag he was carrying and took out two bowler hats and two boiler suits and gave them one of each. They then crossed the room and made their way in the direction of the toilets. There, they passed a door with the silhouette of a female figure with a halo over its head, passed another, but of a male, and then stopped outside a third door that had a silhouette of a winged angel. The chief of security looked quickly left and right, Henry and Herbert followed suit, before all three entered swiftly.

Inside, after they had changed into their new Clothes Henry did a quick double take. There were three urinals, but these were fixed some five feet up a wall. He looked up, then down to his waist, then up again.

"Excuse me," he said to the security chief. "I know this is probably going to sound a silly question..." he pointed up at the urinals; the chief nodded.

"Built different to us..."

"Good grief! They must be if they can reach up there!"

"No," Herbert said. "What he means is Angels don't like, function like the rest of us..." He lifted an arm and pointed to his armpit.

"What...you mean they er pee from there?"

"Correct squire. They don't have a dangly bit like the rest of us that sometimes has a mind of its own...helps them to keep on the celestrial straight and narrow like..."

"Well I never!"

"No, I'm sure you never."

The security chief then reached into a pocket in his gown and removed a small bottle containing some white pills. "Just in case you get into difficulty," he said casually. Henry's eyes narrowed.

"They better not be suicide pills," he

said firmly to Herbert.

"Course not!" Herbert said, before turning to the security chief and adding, "Are they?"

"No, they're quick dissolving knock out pills," Parker said. "Just pop 'em into someone's drink and you'll get plenty of time to skedaddle." Henry pulled a wry face.

"Oh right, so if some bloody great demon gets his claws into us all we have to do is offer to buy him a drink... and no problem." The security chief shrugged.

"Best we could come up with at short notice," he said, passing the bottle to Herbert who pocketed it as the man strode over to a blank wall and touched a certain tile. Immediately there was a faint whirring sound as of an electric motor starting up and twenty seconds later a section of the wall slid back to reveal a lift complete with operator.

"Ernie," Parker said, "Take these two down to the sub-basement."

"Aye aye boss," the operator replied, adding a smart salute.

They were ushered into the lift and just before the door closed they saw the security chief place a hand over his heart and intone: "Tis a far, far, better thing they do now than they ever did before the fickle finger of fate writ and..."

"That sounds suspiciously like a eulogy

to me!" Henry said as the door slowly closed.

**

The lift door opened and Henry and Herbert stepped cautiously out to find that they were in another Gents convenience. Henry glanced at the urinals that were situated in the normal place. "Well", he said, "At least things don't look out of the ordinary here." Herbert shook his head.

"I wouldn't stand too close if I were you squire, we are in..." his words were interrupted then by a loud 'whooshing' sound as a tsunami like wave of water, erupted from the urinal and almost drowned Henry. "...Purgatory after all..." Herbert finished.

Henry groaned, flapped at his boiler suit, took his bowler hat off and shook it, before slapping it back on his head in annoyance.

"Aye," Ernie intoned. "Tis a dire place to be sure. A twilight world where souls hang suspended...neither one nor t'other." Henry took a deep breath.

"Well thank you very much Ernie for those lovely parting words." Ernie nodded.

"Parting? Aye you may very well be right," he said as the lift door closed.

They emerged cautiously into a dimly lit corridor. "Nobody about," Henry

whispered, before adding "Which way?"
Herbert shrugged.

"Don't make much difference," he said
blandly.

"What do you mean, 'don't make
much difference'?"

"Purgatory. Things kind of tend to shift
around a bit down here."

"Left then," Henry decided. They set
off down the drab battleship grey walled
corridor passing a few dull eyed, grey robe
clad people who totally ignored them. After
ten minutes and several turnings to the left
and right they approached a door. It had the
word 'Gentlemen' stencilled on it. "Oh
shhh...it!" Henry groaned. "We're back
where we started!"

"Figgers," Herbert said calmly.

They set off again. This time Henry
said "Let's take opposite turnings to before."
Herbert shook his head.

"No, I don't think so, remember what I
said about things shifting around, we keep to
the same route as before."

A few minutes later they turned a
corner to find themselves in a relatively well
lit open area where they spotted a man sat at
a desk who seemed to be totally engrossed in
reading from a book that looked to be about
as thick as a loaf of sliced bread.

They strode into the room – not aware

that behind them a mystery hand edged itself around the corner they had just turned.

"Come on," Herbert said softly. "And leave the talking to me... Good morning squire," he said cheerily. The man continued with his reading. Then without looking up said: "Is it?"

"What, good?"

"No, morning."

"Oh yeah, don't make much difference down here does it?" The man continued reading.

"Good book is it?"

"Terrible..."

"Not a page turner then..." The man closed the book keeping a finger on the page he was reading.

"United Kingdom Tide Tables, Volume 23, 1927- 1936" Herbert said slowly. "See what you mean squire. Penance is it?" The man nodded.

"Right then squire, we'll leave you to it then; if you wouldn't mind directing us to Central Records."

"Hard to say," the reader said without looking up. "Yesterday, second left, first right, first left...today, who knows."

"Well, that was a lot of use wasn't it?" Henry said glumly as they left.

"Maybe. What did he say, second left, first right, first left?"

"Right."

"What first right last?"

"No you said first left... right."

"Jesus Henry!" Herbert said, before clasping his hands together, looking upward and murmuring "Sorry," before taking a deep breath.

"So, what if we reverse it and go first right, first left, second right?" he said slowly. Henry shrugged.

They set off and soon discovered that the 'Fuck 'em Fairy' was in a playful mood.

"This is beyond a joke," Henry muttered as an hour later they were still tramping down corridors.

"Maybe the next turning," Herbert said in a one in a million hopeful tone of voice. They turned a corner and Bingo! The first door they came to carried bold capital lettering that stated: **'CENTRAL RECORDS'**.

They pushed the door open and entered; without noticing the mystery hand that edged around the last corner they had turned.

Chapter 7

The large room was empty, but for a half dozen chairs that sat in front of a wall mounted large flat screen television and a small radio on a table in one corner.

"What's this then?" Henry said. "Doesn't look like a Records room to me!"

"No," Herbert agreed. "Just hang on a minute while I check something..." He opened the door fully and read the lettering on its outside. It stated: '**TV/RADIO ROOM**'. The 'Fuck 'em' Fairy was at it again and in unison they both muttered "Purgatory..."

"Don't know about you squire," Herbert said wearily as he shut the door, "but I'm done in. Need to put me feet up for a while."

"Right, me too," Henry said as he casually picked up a remote control from one of the chairs, before sinking wearily onto the seat. He idly pointed the control at the TV screen and pressed a red button. The screen came to life showing a cricket match in progress with a boring droning commentary voice in the process of saying: "And that's a single off the last ball of the

389th over, moving the West Indies on to a score of 2,649 for no wickets…" The view then panned to a scoreboard that showed England all out for 24 runs. Henry thumbed the channel button and the scene changed to an old snooker match where Terry Griffiths was addressing the cue ball. Behind him Eddie Charlton is leaning on his cue, apparently asleep.

Griffiths straightens up and walks around the table, before addressing the cue ball again, before straightening up again to take another slow stroll around the table. Eddie Charlton is now snoring.

The commentator whispered: "This absorbing match is now entering its 16th hour – and it couldn't be any tighter, with the score standing at two reds each in this first frame."

Henry yawned and thumbed the channel button again. Terry Wogan filled the screen. Henry pressed the button again. Terry Wogan filled the screen. Henry pressed the button again. Terry Wogan filled the screen. "Arrrggghh!" Henry yelled as he hurled the remote at the offending screen; which shattered and showered a dozing Herbert with bits of glass.

"What the fuck!" Herbert shouted.

"It was horrible!" Henry said in mitigation. Herbert made a 'calm down' gesture.

"Easy...easy squire...It couldn't have been that bad..."

"You didn't see it..."

"No, and not likely to now am I..." Herbert muttered as he brushed a few shards of glass from his lap before his eyes lit on the radio in the corner. "Bit of soothing music," he said, "to calm your nerves?"

"Right, good idea," Henry said as he got up from his chair and switched the radio on, to hear a voice "...welcome our listeners to the Tony Blackburn Joke Show. And here he is the Master of Mirth himself Tonnnee Black..."

Henry changed channels. And another voice said "And what have you been doing today Nookie Bear?"

"That little panda..." said Nookie.

"Nookie! That's not a nice thing to say in front of the children!"

"Sod the feckin' children..." Henry quickly changed channels and was rewarded with gentle bird song.

"Ah, that's better," he said as he returned to his chair just as the bird song faded and a dull voice intoned "This is the third programme in a series of 63, where we examine the life cycle of the Australian Fruit Fly." Henry leapt to his feet, rushed over to the radio and with a manic gleam in his eyes, lifted it over his head.

"Whoa squire! Steady! Calm down now. After all it's only Pur..." Herbert said before Henry finished his sentence for him.

"Gatory...Yes, Yes I know. Sorry... Sorry. Okay now..."

"Good man...Be British...Be British..." Before he could say anything else Herbert was interrupted by the opening of the door and the entry of a man with a gloomy look on his face. Herbert threw out a quick "Excuse me squire," to the man, "but could you direct us to Central Records?"

"This is Central Records," the man muttered. Puzzled, Henry and Herbert glanced at each other. "Wait a minute," Herbert said quietly as watched by Henry, he strode over to the door and opened it. "Central Records," he said before adding a heavy sigh. He turned back into the room and blinked in surprise. It was suddenly full of grey clad people moving among filing cabinets or sitting at desks engrossed in paperwork.

"What?" Henry said noting the puzzled look on Herbert's face. Herbert pointed over Henry's shoulder and Henry turned.

"What the..." Henry muttered. Herbert sighed.

"Are you going to say it or should I?"

"One, two, three, together now," Henry said tiredly.

"Purgatory!"

"C'mon," Herbert said. "Let's see what we can make of this before the bloody thing changes back again." Together they made their way over to the centre of the room where a woman with her back turned was getting something out of a filing cabinet.

"Scuse me miss, but could you assist us?" Herbert said. The woman turned and Henry's brow suddenly creased in concentration. She was, somehow, familiar.

He took in the chestnut hair that had a slight kink in it and was parted in the middle, before it cascaded down onto her shoulders.

Her heart shaped face, widely spaced blue eyes and cute little nose then sparked a youthful memory into glorious life.

"Wanda! Wanda Wrigglesworth!" he exclaimed. "Is it really you!"

"What?" Said Herbert.

"It is...It is you... Isn't it?" Henry said. The light of recognition dawned in the woman's eyes.

"Henry! Henry Pratt! Is that you?"

"Yes, it's me!" Herbert looked from one to the other.

"Whoa, hold on, I'm getting dizzy here, do you two know each other?" Henry grinned.

"Certainly, we were childhood sweethearts!" Henry's face then suddenly clouded. "But what are you doing here Wanda...It wasn't, you know, anything to do with behind that bike shed that time was it?" Wanda smiled.

"No, course not silly we were only ten! It was just down to some minor indiscretions later in life."

"Thank goodness!" Henry said. "I wouldn't like to think that I was responsible..."

"Aw, that's sweet! You always were such a nice quiet boy...well, except for the time behind the bike shed! Anyway I might ask you the same question. What are you doing here?" Before Henry had a chance to answer, Herbert butted in.

"Pardon me miss but my colleague and I are here on official matters to conduct some business."

"Business, what business?"

"We have to check the books."

"What for?" Herbert tapped the side of his nose.

"It's a security issue and top secret." Henry nodded.

"That's right Wanda, so if you can spare the time we'd really appreciate it."

"Time?" Wanda said slowly. "Oh yes, I can spare the time. I've got, let me see, a hundred and seventy two years three months twelve days and..." she looked at her watch, "five hours and sixteen minutes..."

"Wow!" Herbert said "That's some *minor indiscretions*." Henry shot Herbert a withering look.

"You poor girl," he said sympathetically. "Perhaps I can find a way to help you." Wanda forced a wan smile. Herbert shook his head slowly.

"Excuse me *Henry*, but we are here on *official* business y'know. So you get the young lady to show you the books, while I go and see to the *other* business while you are doing that." Herbert's words seemed to sail over Henry's head.

"Pardon?" he said dragging his puppy dog eyes away from Wanda's baby blues.

Herbert sighed and shook his head again.

"Er, the *other* business... remember?"

"Oh, right. Right you go and see to the *other* business then Herbert, while I look over the books with Wanda..."

"Oh yes, good idea Henry. I'll go and do that little thing! I'll be back as soon as I can...Purgatory permitting...Now watch your step and remember... *official* business." Henry nodded firmly.

"Nuff said," he replied as, copying Herbert, he tapped the side of his nose.

Herbert sighed deeply as he left the room.

Henry cleared his throat. "Right Wanda we'll take a look at the Arrivals and Departures books first."

"Certainly Henry, they are right over there behind those cabinets," she said pointing to the other side of the room which was unpopulated and it must be said, rather poorly lit.

"Good," Henry managed before his arm was grabbed and he was almost dragged over to and behind the aforementioned cabinets. A minute later, anyone who happened to be passing would have heard:

"What! WANDA! Not the bike shed you know...You'll get another thousand years!" That same person, if he/she *had* actually passed would also have seen the strange sight of a bowler hat levitating slowly into the air, before a hand reached up and dragged it back down.

Chapter 8

Jesus put an ear to the cold steel of the locked door and listened for half a minute. "Can't hear anything," he whispered to Joan who was standing at his side. She nodded.

"Best if You knock anyway before You unlock it." Jesus nodded and knocked.

"Dad, it's Me I'm going to unlock the door so we can come in to visit..." There was silence for ten seconds before:

"WE? Is that French cow with you!"

"Yes Dad, Joan's here...and y'know she only has Your interests at heart..."

"She can fuck off...She's not stabbing Me again with that bloody needle!" Jesus grimaced.

"Sorry about that Joan," he whispered. Joan shrugged as Jesus continued.

"Now, Y'know You don't mean that Dad..."

In response there was a clap of thunder from inside the room followed by an enormous bang as a lightning bolt smashed into the steel door causing it to vibrate madly.

Joan, who had an ear pressed against the door, leaped back in alarm as the hair on her head suddenly sprang to attention and did a fair impression of a dead dandelion decorated with pretty blue dancing and crackling electrical sparks.

"Dad!" Jesus said reproachfully as He quickly patted out what threatened to be a fire. "You really shouldn't have done that! It nearly set Joan's hair alight!"

"Good, French cow shouldn't have had her head against the door earwigging!" Jesus sighed heavily.

"Better give Me the needle Joan," He whispered. "And it's best if you leave Him to Me..."

"Right Sir," Joan said, "I'll leave You to it while I see if I can get an emergency slot at the hairdressers..."

Jesus watched Joan leave then turned back to the now non-vibrating steel door.

"Right Dad, Joan's gone and it's just Me...I'm coming in," He said before placing, very carefully, the hypodermic in one of His robe's pockets. He turned the heavy key, removed it from the lock and placing it in another pocket, He pushed the door open and entered.

"Right, it's just Me Pater!" He said in a carefully pleasant and modulated tone of voice. "How are You today?" the Boss, who was sat at a little table where He had apparently been reading the latest copy of the

Heaven Herald, narrowed His eyes.

"Where's that French cow then!" He said slowly. Jesus sighed.

"Joan's gone Dad. I think You have offended her."

"Tough Titty!" the Boss said as Jesus sighed again, before changing the subject.

"Anyway; You didn't answer my question; are You feeling a little better today?"

"Better than what?" Jesus pulled a wry face.

"Well, better than yesterday; y'know, the plague of frogs thing..." God shrugged.

"God is as God does," He said.

"I get that Dad, but y'know that whole plague thing from a vengeful God is really a little bit...well, old hat y'know...Old Testament and all that." God frowned.

"Where did You learn to talk like that?"

"Like what?"

"Like *'All that'* *'y'know'*, that's like what!" Now it was Jesus' turn to frown.

"Language changes Dad, we all have to adapt and move on..."

"Oh yes, like doing away with the *Book of Life* and bringing in those bloody computer thingies and floppy dicks... like that you mean?"

"Oh, Peter's been bending Your ear

again has...what floppy dicks?"

"Those thingies you slip into some slot or other in those computer thingies...I think. And yes he did mention the changes..." Jesus took a deep breath.

"Well, increased numbers of admissions were causing a huge backlog; what with the population explosion taking place down there. We needed to embrace technology..."

God "Harrrummphed." Jesus shook his head slowly. This OTT Old Testament phase was proving to be a bit of a bugger.

He took another deep breath.

"And, Your golfing partner, Lucy, is not helping things either. One of our turnstile operators told me that he heard that Lucifer is down on earth as we speak, helping to spread even more grief in the Middle East!"

"The Devil is as the Devil does."

"I get that also Dad, but I do wish You would have a word with him when You have Your next game of golf...which incidentally, is on Thursday I believe. So, we have to get You out of this plague phase. The golf course is a trifle larger than Your living quarters and the sudden appearance or ten ton of bloody locusts on the fairway is going to really piss off the green keepers."

God nodded slowly.

"Well, yes, I suppose it would..."

"So, can we agree that there will be no more plagues of creepy crawlies then?" God Nodded and Jesus took a relieved breath.

"Good, I knew You would see sense... but just to help You get rid of the Old Testament phase a little quicker..." Jesus whipped the needle from his pocket and jabbed it into God's arm.

"Owww! Bastard!" God yelled.

"Just a little prick Dad. There, done now..."

"Little prick! I'll give you little prick!" God shouted, as rubbing His arm He glared at His Son.

Jesus wisely backed up sharply and from a distance of a yard or two waited for whatever was coming next. God took a couple of deep breaths.

It's okay, Jesus thought*; looks like He's not going to explode!* He smiled lightly as His Father then said softly while still rubbing His arm:

"Tell me Son, are You familiar with *Exodus Chapter 9 verses 8 to 12*?" Jesus frowned lightly.

"Well, yes Dad, but to be perfectly honest, they don't spring immediately to mind..." God shook His head and tutted.

"Well then, let me refresh your memory: '*God said to Aaron and Moses Take handfuls of soot from a furnace and have Moses toss it into the air in the presence of pharaoh.*

It will become dust over the whole land of Egypt.

And festering boils will break out on men and animals throughout the land.'"

"And?"

"Well, I just promised that there would be no more plagues of creepy crawlies didn't I?" Jesus nodded.

"And of course Your word is Your bond, isn't it Pater." God nodded.

"It is Son...It is...But cop for this... bastard!" And with a throwing motion towards Jesus' head, a boil roughly the size of Mount Vesuvius magically sprouted on the end of his Son's nose.

"Arggh!" Jesus yelled as his eyes crossed in an effort to view the angry red and purple tipped monstrosity.

"Little Prick!" God said coolly.

Chapter 9

Herbert muttered to himself as he trudged down corridors and stopped to scratch his head at intersections. "Left or right?" he said each time before shrugging lightly and just following his instinct and his nose wherever it took him.

"Now then" he said glancing round a slightly familiar looking section, "The chief said to check out 'Supplies', and if I remember rightly it should be somewhere around here..." As he spoke, a slight shiver suddenly ran down his spine. It was one of those feelings that sometimes whispered in your inner ear: 'you are not alone'. He spun around quickly... nothing, just an empty corridor behind him.

"Just a bit of nervous tension," he muttered as another tiny tremor run up and down his spine and he wriggled his shoulders.

He turned and carried on around a corner and seconds later the fingers of a mystery hand edged around the same corner.

He walked on for five minutes before noticing a door on the left. As he drew up to it he saw that it carried the words *French*

Lessons' and below in smaller letters *'Satisfaction Assured'*.

A smirk blossomed on his face "French Lessons, my arse!" he said. "I remember those types of advertisements in phone booths! And the only lessons on offer there were 'ooh la la' ones!"

He hesitated for a second. He was on serious official business; but what harm would it do. There was nobody around and a short innocent (and hopefully pleasant) diversion wouldn't cause any problems.

He reached for the door handle, turned it and entered a small ante room furnished with a single table that had a hand bell sat on top of it. He rubbed his hands together, picked up the bell and gave it a lusty swing. Seconds later a door opened and a pneumatically proportioned young brunette wearing a mortar board and gown over black bra, stockings, a red suspender belt and killer heels, entered. She was carrying a cane which she swished.

"Bon jour Cherie. Can I per'aps 'elp you?" she said. Herbert grinned.

"Mercy blow through!" he replied running his eyes over her superstructure.

"Ah, so you speak already zee little Francais!"

"Wee a soup son darlin', a soup son..." She pouted seductively and gave her cane another couple of swishes.

"Naughty boy! Come, I will teach you much more." His grin widened.

"Kel bloody bon! I bet you will darlin', I bet you will!" he replied, rubbing his hands together again.

He followed her through the door she had entered...and stopped dead in his tracks. He was in a classroom, and in it, sat at miniature school desks, were half a dozen terrified looking men dressed in school uniforms. And more! Stood facing him in front of a blackboard was a huge woman with a lesbian crop of grey hair who was dressed in what looked very much like a man's dark grey tweed jacket and trousers and carrying a thick bamboo cane.

About the only thing that hinted at 'woman' to him was the fact that she wore four gold wedding bands on the fingers of her left hand. Then part of his sub conscious stepped in and said: *'Not gold; brass...and not rings...knuckle duster...dumbo...'*

"Oh my God!" Herbert murmured (forgetting to raise his eyes and apologise).

"Ah, we have a new pupil. Another seeker of... knowledge...Come in Boy!" the woman demanded. Herbert tried to swallow, but his mouth had suddenly gone dry.

"Er...well thanks for the offer Miss," he said as he began to back out of the room...

"But I just remembered I have to..." His tactical retreat was then blocked by a firm poke in the back from the cane of the pneumatic decoy, who prodded him forward towards a vacant desk.

"You will sit!" the huge woman demanded.

"Yes Miss," Herbert said as he cowered down onto the tiny chair.

"And you will learn...RIGHT!"

"Yes Miss."

"Oui, not Yes...what is it?"

"Wee, wee, Miss!"

"Bon, Tres Bon...BECAUSE IF YOU DO NOT!" She roared, slapping her cane down on the top of his desk, making him jump a foot in the air; "Ve haff vays of makink you very sorry!" And in his panic the fact that she had suddenly swapped nationalities didn't even register.

The traitorous decoy then advanced on his desk and dumped a school blazer, a tie and short trousers in front of him. He gave her a look that would probably have killed her (If she had not been dead already) and muttered to himself "Bloody Purgatory."

***

The door opened and Herbert's bowler-hatted head slowly emerged. He looked cautiously left then right. The coast clear, he stepped out into the corridor; still dressed in blazer, tie, short trousers and carrying his boiler suit. "Bloody sadist!" he moaned as he pulled the door shut, reached a hand behind him and wincing, gently rubbed his nether regions, before adding:

"French Lessons! Satisfaction Assured...Yeah if you're a bloody maso...maso...a kinky swine!"

On the long and winding road back in the direction (he hoped) of relative sanity, he changed back into his boiler suit and dumped the school attire. He also stopped outside a door and jubilantly cried "Yesss!" as he read the large capital lettering that said 'SUPPLIES'. There were two lines of smaller lettering below it and when he squinted to read the first one, his "Yesss!" Became an "ARRRGGHH!" It said: 'Closed for auditing.' He didn't bother to read the second line, which if he had, would have apprised him of the fact that 'Supplies' had been relocated to 'Central Records'.

***

Foot sore and definitely not fancy free, he eventually stood outside a door marked 'CENTRAL RECORDS'. He took a deep breath. "Please!" he said in the fervent hope that the 'Fuck 'em Fairy' was on her lunch break.

He opened the door slowly and breathed a sigh of relief Central Records was still Central Records. He entered the apparently empty room and whispered "Henry, are you in here?" No reply. He was about to ask the question again, but in a much louder voice, when from over behind some filing cabinets he heard what he took to be a female giggle.

"HENRY!" he yelled. There was a scuffling sound like someone scrambling to their feet and a bowler hat appeared over the top of one of the cabinets and was followed by a familiar head.

"Sorry to disturb you...See you're busy like with important business," Herbert said with more than a little pinch of caustic soda in his voice.

"Not at all," Henry said. "We were just killing time till you got back..."

"I've heard it called a lot of things, 'killing time' was never one of them. Anyway," he continued in a business like tone of voice. "Couldn't get a lead on our man down at Supplies, the bloody place was closed for auditing."

"Yes, I know," Henry said casually."

"What! How could you know that, when you've been *occupied* here since the time when I left?"

"One of their admin staff came in about an hour ago and said they were relocating to this office in a couple of days." Herbert took a deep breath and then began slowly counting. "One...Two...Three..."

"Why are you counting?"

"Why? Because in ten seconds I'm going to go fuckin' ape shit! That's why!"

"Herbert! Language in front of a lady!" Henry said, as Wanda, straightening her dress, emerged from behind the filing cabinets.

"Er, excuse the French miss..." Herbert said, before for some reason he stopped and a manic laugh burst from his lips.

"Why on ear... in Purgatory, are you laughing like that?" Henry asked. Herbert shook his head

"Oh, you wouldn't really believe it if I told you squire; so let's just put it down to nervous tension. Anyway, no luck at Supplies, so it looks like I failed."

"Well I didn't," Henry said with a grin on his face.

"Yeah, I can see that," Herbert said, looking directly at Wanda.

"No! Not that," Henry said. "You went looking for a man, when we should have been looking for a woman!" He and Wanda then exchanged very meaningful looks before grinning.

"Bloody Hell Henry! What's got into you, you randy little so and so! I leave you for a couple of hours and you turn into a raving sex maniac!"

"No! What I meant was our contact is a woman!"

"A woman!"

Henry smiled then made a point of nodding firmly in Wanda's direction. Herbert blinked.

"What? You mean your Wanda...Your Wanda is the contact we are looking for?"

"Yep."

"You sure?

"Yep. While you were away I kind of accidentally exposed myself and..."

"Bloody Hell, he's at it again!"

"My halo I mean! She saw my halo and then it all came out...like."

"And she gave you the right response?"

"I'll say!"

"She- gave-you-the-secret code-phrase." Herbert said slowly and wearily.

"Yes. Cobblers' Awls..." Herbert nodded.

"Thank you Henry. And welcome to the Club Wanda."

She smiled and nodded. "Thank you Herbert. And if you boys come with me I'll take you to the secret lift that will whisk us down to *The Basement*," she said, glancing around the room to make sure they were alone.

They followed her into what turned out to be a large strong room that was lined on three walls with steel shelving that held cardboard boxes. Curious, Henry slid one out and said "What's this then?"

"Long term guests," Wanda replied as Henry read the box's title "Genghis Kahn and," he read a line of text below the title, "Release Date: first of the sixth, two thousand three hundred and eighty five. Phew!" He slid the box back onto the shelving and picked up another one. "Caligula: Release Date: thirty first of the first three thousand four hundred twenty seven. My word!" he said as he put the box back, before a thought struck him. "These people; surely they all seem to be prime candidates for *The Basement*. How come they ended up in Purgatory instead of down *There*?" Wanda nodded.

"Well yes, in the normal course of events they would have been nailed on for the drop; but they had the excuse of being on earth before any of the major religions got around to telling them how to behave...so they got a get out of jail card, so to speak."

As she finished Wanda ducked behind a row of shelving. "Won't be a minute," she said. "I'm just changing into something more appropriate."

"Women!" Herbert muttered to himself.

True to her word, Wanda re-appeared quickly. She had changed out of her dowdy clerks outfit into a black clingy *very* mini skirt and a tight red scoop neck t-shirt that left *very* little to the imagination. Seeing the surprised looks on Henry and Herbert's faces she said evenly: "Standard dress for women down there. Don't want to look out of place."

Wanda moved over to the end of a rack of shelving, reached up and pulled out a box that had nothing written on it. "This one is of no interest, so it never gets moved." She said, before leaning forward and touching a particular spot on the backing wall. There was a loud click followed by the whirling of machinery and within seconds a section of the empty wall slid back to reveal a lift.

"Right gents," she said softly, "I suggest you unbutton your collars...it's going to get plenty hot..."

Chapter 10

Henry's knees buckled and his stomach, which had taken up residence in his throat decided it preferred its previous abode and did a quick flit back to somewhere above his hips as the plunge came to an abrupt halt.

The old (pre death) Henry would almost certainly, at the outset of that plunge yelled "Ohhhh Sugarrrr!" But the post death Henry was in some respects, a different man. Now he just said: "Wooo! That was some ride!"

The shift from an 'Ohhhh Sugarrrr!' Henry to the more urbane, 'Hey I'm a Cool Dude' Henry had been born (pre death) with the discovery that he was not a total wimp devoid of any manly attributes.

He had boldly tackled the fearsome *Harakiri*... Well, okay, he hadn't *actually* taken the beast on one hundred percent willingly; but he had placed himself in the position to do just that by finding out that he had an innate skill.

And anyway, although that other 'descent' did begin with a long drawn out "Argh!" and an "Oh Sugar!" It had ended (just before the SMACK) with a prematurely cut off bold "You can do it!"

The lift door slid open to reveal a large and dimly lit room that was almost full of huge piles of yellow powder.

"Sulphur?" Henry said, as he took in the pungent smell. Wanda shook her head.

"Well, that is the modern name for it, but down here it goes by the more archaic name of 'Brimstone', as that sits well when tagged on to the 'Fire' bit."

Herbert strode over to a door and cautiously opened it a crack to peer out.

"Looks okay," he whispered, before opening the door fully and stepping out into a narrow corridor. Henry and Wanda followed and together they set off in the direction of muted noises that sounded like the scraping of many shovels against stone flooring.

As they travelled down the corridor the air became increasingly hotter until they began to have trouble breathing and tiny pearls of sweat began to bead their foreheads.

"My G...goodness," Henry gasped. "How in ...the other place; do they cope with this heat!" Herbert looked at him and shrugged lightly.

"I suppose the same way you used to cope with the rain in Manchester..."

Henry was about to ask if perhaps his companion haled from the other side of the Pennines, in Yorkshire, where sheep

bothering was the number one pastime...
when they turned a corner and walked slap
bang into a scene straight from...well Hell.

They stood on the edge of a cavernous
room, the ceiling of which lay 'somewhere,
above a hazy cloud of yellowish smoke and
super heated air.

At one side of the room they saw four
enormous furnaces, with mouths wide open
displaying their fiery throats and demanding
food. In front of them stood a large circle of
black boiler-suited men with sweat and dirt
grimed faces, who were carrying huge
shovels.

In the middle of the circle was a single
man who was addressing them.

"And I say to you brothers," the man
shouted, "YOU HAVE RIGHTS! Stand up
for them AND TOGETHER WE CAN
WIN!"

The man balled his hands into fists,
and then raised his arms on high as though
about to call upon a higher power; which
really was a bum call, considering where they
stood.

"WHAT'S GOING ON HERE?" The
strident words echoed round the huge room,
causing the man and his assembled audience
to turn quickly towards the speaker. It was a
late middle aged woman dressed in an SS
uniform and carrying a whip. From his

position on the edge of the room, Henry's eyes opened wide.

"It's Her!" he said.

"Who her?" Herbert said.

"Maggie bloody Thatcher, that's who!"

"Who?"

"After your time maybe, I suppose."

The woman elbowed her way through the circle of men and repeated her question to the speaker. "I said, what's going on here YOU HORRIBLE LITTLE MAN!" The man visibly wilted under the verbal battering.

"Er, we demand changes..." he said meekly.

"Changes...DEMAND...DEMAND CHANGES!" The man swallowed nervously then he rallied slightly.

"Yes. We demand a 120 hour week and...and ten minute lunch breaks..."

"Would you also like some luncheon vouchers too?"

"Er, yes we also demand luncheon vouchers!" he said looking around the assembled men, who mostly half heartedly, nodded in response.

"And how about sick leave...would you like some sick leave...to give your broken bones time to heal?"

"Er, yes we demand sick leave to give our...What broken bones?"

"The broken bones you get when I

have the lot of you stretched on the rack. NOW BACK TO WORK!" This last demand arrived like an electric shock to the goolies and within five seconds the circle of men - and their spokesman- were back shovelling like...Hell; while Gruppenfuhrer Thatcher smiled and said:

"Oh yes; I saw off plenty of others with bigger balls than you lot!"

Stood on the edge of the room Herbert blew his cheeks out "Phew," he said. "That one could give our friend Genghis Khan a run for his money!" Henry nodded.

"You don't know the half of it..."

***

They slid away from the huge room without capturing the attention of the resident harridan - who was busy projecting her evil eye towards the frantically shovelling stokers - and carried on down the corridor for a few minutes before Henry stopped for a second to mop his brow.

"Is it me," he said, "or is it getting even hotter?" Herbert nodded.

"Those furnaces back there probably heat this section of Hell and the way those stokers were shovelling, it's no wonder the bloody place is near to boiling." Henry nodded, ran a finger round his collar and blew out a lungful of hot air.

"Phew!" he said shaking his head. "Don't know about you two, but I could murder an ice cold lager right now." Herbert shook his head.

"Don't think you should have said that squire..." Henry frowned.

"Why not?"

"Cause my friend, in case it has slipped your notice, this is Hell and expressing a desire for something is almost certainly going to lead to big disappointment... at the very least."

No sooner had he spoken, when ten yards ahead, from a side junction, a bikini clad young woman emerged pushing an enclosed trolley that bore a sign saying 'Free Cold Drinks'. Henry grinned.

"Looks like you're wrong this time Herbert! We'll have three cold ones miss!" He said brightly as the woman drew level.

The young woman gave him a dazzling smile, reached into the trolley and pulled out three frost covered bottles.

"See!" Henry said as she handed them over to him. Herbert shook his head slowly as the woman carried on down the corridor.

"Yes, we'll see," he offered to her retreating back.

Henry passed them each a bottle, but then in a puzzled voice said "Er, wait a minute; these bottles don't seem to have a top. There's no opening!"

"No opening!" Herbert said in a mock surprised voice.

"No opening!" Henry confirmed.

"Well I never!" Herbert said as he slowly rolled the chilled bottle across his sweating forehead.

They carried on down the corridor for several minutes before Henry asked Herbert if he actually knew where Hell's laundry room was situated.

"No," Herbert said. "Never had the need to go there during my little excursions in the past; but even if I did, just like Purgatory, it has probably moved around a fair bit since my last visit. .. and anyway, we don't want to 'find it' yet. We've got some ferreting to do first!" Henry nodded.

"Then how about we start here?" he said, pointing to a door that had *'Brimstone Bulletin'* written on it; along with the words *'Proprietors Robert Maxwell / Rupert Murdoch.*

He turned the handle and they entered a dingy room littered with old machinery parts. At the back of the room they saw another door and behind this they heard the clanking of machinery and could just make out what sounded like two men having a heated argument. Henry tip toed over to the door and carefully eased it open a few inches.

The voices became clearer.

"I'm telling you we need new plant, this Caxton press is a pile of shit!" one of the men said, before adding: "With modern equipment we can cut our hours down to 100 a week..."

"Dingo Dust!" The other man replied. "Are you potty Igor! Cut our hours and before you know it we'll be back on the bloody banjos shovellin' coal...dumb fuckin' Slav!"

"Who you calling a dumb fuckin' Slav you antipodean mongrel! You've only been here five fucking minutes and you think you run the fucking place!" The other man smirked.

"Yeah, well, I might be new, but once I've been here as long as you, you dumb fuckin' Slav, I probably will be runnin' the fuckin' place!"

"Oh yeah! Well I think there is someone else around here that'd soon knock the cockiness out of you, you fucking antipodean mongrel!"

"Oh yeah, and... Oh fuck!"

"Oh fuck what?"

"All the fuckin' vowels have disappeared again on the double page spread I've just laid. I'll have to fuckin' lay it all out again!"

"Ah, well, like I said, if we had modern

equipment that wouldn't happen. Fucking Caxton press and lead lettering..."

"Don't fuckin' start that again you dumb fuckin', Slav!"

"Who you calling a dumb fuckin' Slav you antipodean mongrel!"

Henry closed the door softly, turned and shook his head. "Let's move on. We'll get no sense out of those two," he said.

**

The next door they came to had a sign that read '*Accounts – Chief Accountant: Philip Greene.*

Herbert gently inched the door open and peeped inside, to see a large late middle aged and balding man sat at a desk in front of a computer monitor.

"What the Heaven!" the man shouted. "Three hundred pounds for a one night stay at the *Hades Hilton*! What does he take me for? My Devil; he obviously thinks we're made of bloody money!"

Herbert opened the door wider and coughed lightly before saying in an apologetic voice, "Er, excuse me squire..." The man raised his eyes from the screen and frowned.

"Yes; what do you want!"

"Sorry to bother you squire, but my

companions and I are on a special assignment. We're here to tackle the ongoing laundry problem that has been..."

"About time!" the man snorted. "I'm down to my last three clean cashmere sweaters and my hand made monogrammed silk shirts look like something out of bloody Primark. How I'm supposed to keep my appearance up to par I don't know!"

"Quite squire. Anyway, our enquiries lead us to believe that the main problem could lie in the flow return pipes situated near the, er, dungeons. So if you would be so good as to point us in the right direction we would be most..."

"Dungeons? Couldn't say. Not been here that long. Punishment Rooms I know."

"Punishment Rooms? Oh right, that might help us in our..."

"End of corridor, turn right and follow the sound of cracking whips."

"Right squire thanks for..."

"And shut the bloody door on your bloody way out!"

Chapter 11

They followed the sound of cracking whips
(and tortured moans) and soon found
themselves outside a huge black, metal clad
and studded door, that bore the bold and
intimidating legend **PUNISHMENT
ROOMS** and below (in a smaller and less
intimidating type face): *'Your Pain is Our
Pleasure (Please pull knob for entry)'*. Next to the
text was an arrow pointing to a recessed
niche in the wall inside which sat the said
knob.

   Henry swallowed nervously as Herbert
reached out and tugged on the knob ... which
immediately triggered from somewhere
inside, the opening lines of *The Adams Family*
theme music.

   "Nice touch that," Herbert said as the
music died. Henry was not impressed.

   "Nice touch! Bloody macabre, that's
what I call it!" Herbert shrugged.

   "Well, you know, a little light relief
now and again is not a bad thing."

   "Light relief! Here we are swallowed
up in the bowels of Hell about to enter a
bloody Torture Chamber and be dragged into
who knows what kind of barbarity...and it's

'Light Relief!'" Wanda placed a hand lightly on Henry's shoulder.

"It's okay Henry," she said softly. "Hell is new to me too; but I have been dead long enough to be able to adjust to it. You'll eventually readjust too."

Henry took a deep breath, nodded slowly, and was about to say something when, with an ominous creaking the door swung slowly open to reveal a red eyed and horned demon carrying a sinister looking pitchfork.

"Ah!" the demon said flicking a forked tongue over his lips and slowly swishing his long tail. "What have we here then; more miscreants in need of chastisement?" Herbert stepped forward smartly.

"No squire, we're here on official business." The demon's eyes narrowed.

"What official business?" Herbert reached into a pocket of his boiler suit and took out their papers.

"Here you are squire I think you will find them in order." The demon reached out a black nailed clawed hand, took the papers and began to read.

"Looks alright," he muttered. "But you should be at the laundry. What you doing here?"

"Well sir, as you are no doubt aware, there are three main double-header tanks, each with its own self-reticulating primary and secondary vacuum pump system attached, which are themselves feeding into the main supply conduits."

"Er, of course..."

"Yes, and somewhere in the tangential supply web there would appear to be a partial seal collapse that is allowing extraneous foreign matter to be sucked in..."

"Makes sense."

"We think so too. The problem is, where is the breakdown? Our web charts have been misplaced by those fools in *Sector Four*, so we've no way of knowing." Herbert sighed and shrugged his shoulders. The demon sneered.

"Sector Four eh! Well no doubt they'll soon be my guests. I'll teach them to take care of official documents!"

"Too true squire! So, you can see our problem. We've got to check all possible vacuum seal sites and that's why we need to have a good look round here..." Herbert glanced across at Henry and Wanda, both of whom slowly nodded their agreement. The demon mirrored their nods.

"Right then, I'm not too busy at the moment, just finished poking a dozen miscreants in their arses with my trusty pitchfork; so if you will follow me I'll show you around."

"Well okay," Herbert said, "as long as you're not too busy." The demon shrugged.

"Well I do have irons in the fire at the minute..."

"Irons," Herbert said casually. "What irons might they be then?" The demon frowned.

"What?"

"You have some irons in the fire?"

"Yeah, so?"

"Well, I just asked what irons you had in the fire, that's all." The demon frowned again.

"Iron irons," he said slowly.

"Iron irons?" Herbert said.

"Yeah, what did you think...papier mache irons?" Herbert nodded slowly.

"Oh, I see, you meant *actual* irons, not figurative irons!"

"Doh, yeah!" *Actual* irons! I heat 'em up till they're cherry red, then I get the miscreants over a barrel..."

"An actual barrel, you mean, not just a figurative barrel?" The demon took a deep breath.

"A barrel...a fuckin' barrel...okay!"

"Sorry."

"Right, I gets them over an *actual* barrel an says to them 'get ready to receive ten inches of red hot iron up your jaxie...an' then they usually crap themselves..."

"Figuratively?"

"They *actually* crap themselves. Fuckin' Hell am I talkin' double Dutch or what!"

"Sorry, sorry..."

"Yeah right, but this is where, for me, the 'light bulb moment' thing comes in...Is that the right phrase by the way, for a magic moment thingy?" Herbert nodded.

"Er, I think so..."

"Yeah I thought so. Anyway when I sometimes moved the iron real close they'd feel the heat and start *figuratively* crapping themselves again. Then when I repeated it a few times they would almost end up as gibbering wrecks. 'Oh right I thought, this is a bit of *Headology;* maybe I should introduce this to the curriculum.'"

"And did you?"

"Yeah, it's a real blast. You should see the fuckers gibber and squirm! Only downside is, after a dozen or so practice moves they tend to come down off the ceiling a bit thinking they aren't going to get it up 'em...and that's when they get it big time!"

Herbert nodded. "Well, thank you for clearing that up; so please, if you are ready, lead on."

As the demon led the way Henry whispered to Herbert "Where did you get all that technical stuff from, it was brilliant."

"Used to be a plumber and it came in

handy for massaging the bills." Henry blinked.

"So how come you didn't end up down here then?"

"Repented didn't I. And just in time as it happened. Bloody electric cable! Whole bathroom wall for it to be buried in and it had to be in the one place where I drilled...Flash Bang Wallop! Goodnight Vienna!"

"In here," the demon said ahead of them as he opened a door leading into a huge room where a number of pitchfork wielding imps and other demons were prodding and herding a score of men wearing red football tops towards rows of benches set in front of a large cinema sized screen. "Man United supporters," their guide said. "We've got a special short football film for them that runs for 24 hour's non-stop with slowmo and action replays."

The men were forced into seats, their wrists were attached to the chairs' arms by manacles and the screen blinked into life. There was a match taking place. One team was dressed in sky blue the other in a hooped kit. As the camera homed in for a closer shot there was a snarling response from the captives: It was Manchester City in blue, and according to the scoreboard their opponents in hoops were Queens Park

Rangers.

As the significance of this particular match registered the captives began to writhe and the room was suddenly filled with a choice selection of Anglo Saxon swearwords. Henry frowned.

"It's just a football match, what's the big deal?"

"You're not a fan then?" the smiling demon said. Henry shrugged.

"No, not really. Twenty-two men running around after a ball between bouts of falling down and rolling on the grass like they've been machine gunned..."

"Ah well, if you look in the top corner of the screen you will see this game, with only a minute or two to go is almost over and the score is tied."

"So, it looks like nobody wins and it will be a boring draw." The demon grinned and shook his head.

"Let me fill you in on the scenario here. A couple of hundred miles away City's rivals for the League crown, United, have just this minute finished their own last game of the season to leave them three points above City and they are the Champions elect unless City win and thus take the title on a better goal difference."

"So?"

"So watch." Henry turned back to the

game.

One of the men in blue had the ball and was bearing down on the Queens Park Rangers goal. The commentator's voice throbbed with rising excitement – excitement that climaxed with an amazed and almost strangulated "AAGGUUUEROOOOO!" as the player (Aguero, not AAGGUUUEROOOOO!) shot and scored, the referee blew the full time whistle and the assembled captives went berserker bananas (some even foaming at the mouth in impotent rage). Henry shuddered.

"Oh my Go...Goodness, that's nasty!" Herbert shrugged.

"Bradford City fan myself...never had any delusions of grandeur..."

"Ace chastisement, or what!" the demon said proudly. Herbert nodded.

"Probably hurt more than a good prod up the arse with a pitchfork..."

"Exactly! Mental torment! Too many demons are still stuck in the old ways, content with a bit of bloodletting.

"Okay that does provide a quick buzz when they squeal like stuck pigs but I find that the psychological route of *Headology* is much more satisfying as the pain lasts much longer. Hell, stick 'em in the arse and the wound heals again in a matter of minutes..." Henry blinked.

"Heals again in a matter of minutes?" Herbert was quick to step in.

"He's pretty new squire," he said slowly turning to Henry. "Remember our earlier discussion about suicide and such. Not much point of puttin' 'em out of action for a long time with a serious injury that would need time for them to recuperate and heal. Best a quick recovery, so you can give 'em some more pain almost right away."

"Too right!" the demon said. "But," he added, "I still think you can't beat a bit of sophisticated mental anguish. And", he preened proudly, "I've gained a bit of a reputation in that direction." Herbert smiled and nodded.

"Right, so I guess you could call yourself an Innovator."

The demon smiled smugly. "*Innovator*, yeah I like that." Herbert nodded.

"Bet the Boss likes that too; someone with the brains and aptitude to come up with new variations on the theme..." The demon shook his head slowly.

"I suppose he would, but stuck in this arse end of the Sector he's not likely to hear about it."

"Well squire, he will when we meet up to give him our report. We'll make sure we put in a good word for you." The demon was a little taken aback.

"You'd do that for me!" Herbert nodded firmly.

"Course squire. It's the least we can do for your help; so when you're ready, lead on with the tour..."

They followed the demon through a door that led into a short corridor at the end of which was another door with intimidating text over the lintel. This read

Punishment Rooms and underneath, again in a less intimidating type face, *'Mark II Headology'*

"Another one of my little *Innovations* – like that word," he said nodding at Herbert – "where we don't go in for sticking forks in people or roasting them over open fires. Electronics, modern technology... *Headology* again," he said, tapping his temple with a black nailed clawed finger and smiling.

He opened the door, bowed and ushered them through into another large room, the walls of which were lined with what looked to be soundproofed booths each with a door and single window.

Every booth had an occupant who, like the previous captives, was manacled to a chair. But unlike the others, these seemed to be in one of the varying stages of a – teeth gnashing, temple throbbing, eyes bulging, body writhing – descent into a state of total catalepsy.

Their guide strode over to one of the booths and opened the door a few inches and the visitors reeled back as a 120 decibel wave of sound assaulted them between the ears.

"Mister Blobby's number 1 hit," he said proudly. "Played *ad- infinitum.* I've got it piped through on a loop to every booth. Good hey!" Henry shuddered.

"Diabolical!"

"Precisely! Thanks, it gets better though. Come on I'll show you..." They followed him past the poor wretches and through a door to another large room that was also lined with booths each containing a manacled occupant.

"Variation on the theme," he said proudly as he eased the door of a booth open for them to hear an announcer say "Norway Nil Points..." He shut the door quickly.

"It's not..."Henry began; glancing at the almost comatose occupant slumped in his chair.

"Yep! Eurovision Song Contests for the last 30 years, Terry Wogan and all...on another *ad-infinitum* loop! And here's the devilish bit, after a week or two we switch these perps with those in the other room. You should see the *very short lived* looks of relief on their faces when they change over, it's a blast!"

"Any more of these remarkable

innovations?" Henry asked lightly. The demon shook his head and frowned.

"No, not at the minute...but you can be sure I'll come up with plenty more soon!"

"I'll bet you will," Henry said. The demon nodded vigorously.

"Yep; but in the meantime seeing as you all seem to appreciate my efforts I can take you to see some of the more traditional – and to my mind – more prosaic and dare I say it; boring chastisements." The visitors exchanged quick glances before Herbert said,

"Well since there does not appear to be anything in these rooms that could have a bearing on our quest for answers to the laundry problem...lead on McDuff." The demon nodded again.

"Good, we'll go through to the Games Room then."

***

Another large room and just inside the door they read a notice board that laid out the day's activities which included:

11.45 A.M. 'Blindfolded Catch the Javelin'

12.00 Noon 'Pin the Tail on the Tiger'

1.35 P.M. 'Catch the Cobra'

2.45 P.M. 'Forfeits (Arm/Leg/Other)

3.30 P.M. 'Irish Roulette'

Henry read them through and then frowned. "Irish Roulette?" he said. The demon nodded.

"Same as Russian, but with five bullets instead of one..."

"Oh, right, that figgers..." The demon checked his watch.

"Ten to twelve," he said. "The javelin contest will be over now." And as if to confirm his statement a side door opened and two imps entered carrying a man on a stretcher who lay with face deathly white and eyes closed, clutching at the shaft of a javelin that was sticking out of his chest.

"Good effort," one of the imps said in admiration. "He nearly caught it. Should qualify for the final tomorrow."

"The final! Lucky fellow!" Henry said in mock delight. The demon nodded.

"Not all punishment you know...gotta give them something to aim at!"

"So I see," Henry said," looking at the recently well planted javelin.

"The next event starts in a few minutes," the demon said. "So it's probably best if we adjourn to the viewing booth," he said, pointing to a booth at the far end of the room. "It could get a bit messy," he added.

Herbert glanced back at the notice board.

"Pin the Tail on the Tiger," he

mouthed. "And I assume we are talking 'real tiger' here then?"

"Course; not much point otherwise is there?"

"No, I suppose not. But I think," Herbert muttered looking across at Henry's and Wanda's suddenly decidedly pale faces; "as there doesn't seem to be anything in here that looks out of place, perhaps we should move on... quickly?" The demon shrugged.

"If you insist; but you will miss a laugh a minute with this one...if it lasts that long, of course..." Herbert looked at his watch.

"Best we move on squire."

"Oh well, if you insist...one of my favourite's this though...but what the Hell, I suppose I can always catch it tomorrow," the demon said with a trace of disappointment in his voice.

"Right, where to next then?" Herbert said.

"Water Sports. We have an Olympic sized pool you know!"

***

Five minutes later they arrived at another door. This time the day's events were highlighted outside on a board. Henry read: 'Tickle the Piranhas, and 'Race the Crocodiles'.

"Another good one this," the demon enthused. "Except I must confess it does get a little bit boring waiting for the pool to be drained in between heats, particularly the crocodile ones."

"Drained, why?" Wanda asked.

"The water; soon gets a bit cloudy with all the blood; makes it hard to get the full enjoyment from the spectacle." Wanda's already pale face went a couple of shades paler as from inside they heard a loud thrashing of water and a number of horrendous screams.

"Looks like the croc heats have just finished," the demon said with a note of disappointment. "We'll have to wait for the imps to drain and refill the pool."

"Er, how long will that take then?" Herbert asked.

"Oh, about thirty minutes."

"That long, well perhaps," Herbert said glancing at the ashen faces of his companions, "maybe we should move on?" The demon was a little disappointed again.

"Pity," he muttered. Henry chimed in.

"Yes, I'm sure it would have been very entertaining..."

"Laugh a minute..." the demon said.

"But nowhere near as clever and *innovative* as your other brilliant Headology triumphs!" Henry replied. The demon's chest visibly swelled with pride.

"Nice of you to say so...and you won't forget to tell that to the Boss when you see him?"

"You can count on that squire," Herbert said, adding a very firm nod. The demon's chest swelled even further.

"So, where to next?" Henry asked. The demon scratched his head.

"Well really you've seen all there is here...unless you want to wait for the pool to be refilled..." Wanda quickly stepped forward.

"Tempting sir, but come to think of it, if I'm not mistaken, I'm almost sure I spotted a potential trouble spot on the web charts; before those idiots in Sector Four went and lost them." The demon snorted.

"I'm looking forward to seeing them!" Wanda nodded.

"And I bet they'll soon regret their sloppy ways when you introduce them to your brilliant Headology programme!"

"You can say that again!" Henry agreed before adding "Ah yes, now you mention it I also remember that potential trouble spot. It was outside the dungeons wasn't it?" Wanda nodded.

"Yes it was...outside the dungeons..."

"Dungeons?" the demons said

"Yes, you know, where the real perps

are banged up," Herbert chipped in.

"No dungeons in this sector," the demon said firmly. "We only deal with misdemeanours down here."

'Misdemeanours', Wanda thought *'Catch the Javelin, Irish Roulette, Race the bloody Crocodile!* She took a deep breath. "Then where can we find the dungeons sir?"

"Level Sixty-Six."

"Level Sixty-Six?"

"Yeah."

"And how do we get to level sixty-six squire?" Herbert said.

"Back the way you came in, turn first right at the Punishment Rooms, follow the corridor and that brings you to the inter-level express lift."

"Thanks," Herbert said. "You've been most helpful..."

"Whoa! You can't just run off like that!"

"Er, why not?"

"Don't get many non-miscreant guests down here; let me stand you a spot of lunch."

"Thanks," Herbert said, "But we should really be on our way..."

"I INSIST. And anyway, it will give me the chance to showcase another of my subtle little *innovations*." The guests exchanged quick looks before Herbert said "How could we refuse...lead on squire."

Chapter 12

Another five minutes and they found themselves, plates in hand in the Sector Canteen that apart from themselves was empty of anyone else, other than a bored looking demon that was standing on the serving side of the long counter.

"Chicken Madras, Lamb *a la* Vindaloo or Chilli Con Carne," the demon muttered as Herbert approached.

"Lamb *a la* Vindaloo for me... cee vou play." The demon sighed.

"Chicken Madras, Lamb *a la* Vindaloo, Chilli Con Carne?" the demon repeated.

"Er, Lamb *a la* Vindaloo...without the French quip at the end please." The demon gave Herbert a tired look that translated to: *'Think you're a smart arse do you'* before reaching for the handle of a ladle that was sticking out of a slowly bubbling pot.

"Bollocks!" he muttered as he lifted the utensil out of the pot to find that the handle was all that was left of the ladle. "Third fucking one today," he sighed, reaching under the counter for a replacement and plopping a large dollop of dark brown sludge onto Herbert's plate.

"Next," the demon said as Henry moved up.

"I'll pass on the Lamb *a la* Vindaloo," Henry said quickly.

"Chicken Madras or Chilli Con Carne?"

"Chilli Con Carne for me please." The sludge looked suspiciously identical to that on Herbert's plate.

"Next." Wanda reluctantly moved forward.

"Do you have any salad?"

"Chicken Madras, Lamb *a la* Vindaloo, Chilli Con Carne?"

"I think I will have the Chilli please."

The trio made their way over to the table where their friendly neighbourhood demon sat patiently waiting.

"You not dining today squire?" Herbert asked as he sat down. The demon smiled.

"No, not today. You go ahead...and *bon appétit*."

They looked at each other. Herbert shrugged and cautiously took a mouthful of the sludge. A second later his eyes opened wide. "Bloody Hell!" he said. "It's bloody gorgeous!" The demon smiled as Henry and Wanda picked up their eating irons.

Minutes later there were three empty

plates on the table and Herbert belched loudly. "Now that's what I call a curry!" he said. Henry nodded.

"And the Chilli might have looked particularly unappetising but the taste was excellent!" Wanda nodded her agreement.

"Glad you enjoyed it," the still smiling demon said.

"So," Wanda asked, "was that the subtle innovation you mentioned before; making a fabulous meal out of dollops of dark brown sludge?" The demon's smile widened.

"You could say that. Anyway, duty calls and I'll leave you now. Oh and by the way I'm sure you'll want to wash your hands before you go. The washrooms are over to the right."

He rose to his feet and with a little bow (and a smile) he left.

"You know," Henry said looking towards the retreating demon's back, "He's not so bad really... for a demon." Herbert was about to agree but he was stopped by a sudden volcanic rumbling from his stomach.

"Whoops, manners, excuse me!" he said. Seconds later another Versuvial rumble brought a frown to his face. "Y'know?" he said getting quickly to his feet, "I think I will go and...wash my hands...right now!" Henry and Wanda's faces suddenly mirrored

Herbert's frown and Henry gently slid his chair backwards.

"Er, yes," he muttered, "I think that's a good idea, excuse me Wanda."

"I think I will go with you..." Wanda said softly in reply. They followed Herbert's bum cheek clenching gait to the washrooms where they split up, Wanda entering the 'Ladies' and the men the 'Gents'.

Inside the toilets Herbert made a beeline for the nearest cubicle. It was locked.

"Arrgghh Shit!" he yelled. "The fucking thing is locked!"

Henry, a pace behind him, fetched up at the second cubicle.

"Look!" he said pointing to a small sign that said 'Lock Pick' next to a piece of string with a safety pin attached, that was dangling from a nail at the side of each door.

"Oh fuck...Oh fuck!" Herbert moaned, as he danced up and down on the spot.

Five minutes later a very delicate looking pair of ex-diners emerged from the Gents to find an equally delicate looking companion standing outside the Ladies.

"Lock Pick?" Henry asked

"Bastard!" Wanda replied.

"Not so bad really...for a demon!" Herbert said sourly looking at Henry.

***

The sign said *'Inter-Level Express'* (in suitable 'go-faster' bold italics). Herbert strode forward and pressed the down arrow button and within 30 seconds they heard a whooshing sound followed by a soft sighing of hot air being forced out through the slight gap at the foot of the door, which slid silently open. Henry swallowed nervously. "Level sixty-six," he muttered. "That's a long way down isn't it?" Herbert shrugged.

"Up, down, sideways. What's the difference?" Henry shook his head.

"The difference; to me anyway, is that sixty-six floors down represent the *Bowels of Hell*. And that means there is an awful long way up before we can get out of it." Wanda stepped forward.

"Come on then you two. We've come this far, once more into the breach..."

"Oh great," Henry muttered. "Charge of the bloody *Light Brigade*...and we know what happened to them..."

They entered, the door slid closed and Henry's mind conjured up an image of a steel tomb. He was about to say something when Wanda reached a hand out towards a large bank of numbered buttons on a side wall of the *tomb*, pressed '66'; and the floor beneath their feet fell away.

"Owww!" Henry yelled as his head hit the ceiling and his stomach plummeted to somewhere near his feet. Herbert and Wanda, who had been holding onto side rails reached up with their free hands and dragged him down.

"You shoulda held on," Herbert said casually. "It is an Express lift you know."

Henry made a very conscious effort to force the remainder of his Chilli Con Carne back down into his stomach from its present position just behind his front teeth. He was helped considerably twenty seconds later when his knees buckled and his body folded south to leave him kneeling on the floor as the freefall suddenly stopped.

"We're there," Wanda said.

"You don't say," Henry managed before adding. "I think I am developing a phobia about lifts..."

The door slid open and they emerged into a high dimly lit bare stone walled cavern.

"C'mon then," Wanda said loudly, "Let's take a good look around." Herbert cringed.

"Shhh!" he whispered urgently.

"Why are you whispering?" Henry said. "There's nobody around, look."

"Yeah, well say you don't know... walls have ears, an' all that..."

With Wanda in the lead they set off down a number of grim passageways without meeting any of Hell's denizens along the

way; before she pulled up sharply. "Shhh!"
she said.

"What! What!" Henry said.

"Shhh!" Herbert replied.

"Sorry," Henry whispered.

"I thought I heard music." Wanda
said.

"Music?" Herbert said.

"Shhh!" Wanda said. "Listen, there it
is again."

"She's right, it is...it's pop music!"
Henry mouthed.

They exchanged quick glances before
setting off in the direction that the music
seemed to be coming from and soon found
themselves standing outside a large metal
door with the word **Donjons** spelt out in
thick square headed bolts on it.

"It's definitely coming from in there,"
Henry said softly before knocking gingerly.
They waited for a very long minute.

"Knock again," Wanda said. Henry
knocked more loudly. Another minute
dragged by.

"Try the door," Wanda said. Henry
took a deep breath and tried the handle.
There was an ominous creak as the heavy
door inched open and a blast of sound – that
resolved itself into Madonna singing *Like a
Virgin* – assaulted their ears. Henry opened
the door wider and they found themselves

looking into a large room furnished with a huge black leather chesterfield, a matching arm chair, a black, glass topped coffee table and what appeared to be a drinks cabinet; all of which sat on a blood red fitted carpet.

The walls of the room were painted a matt black that was tastefully relieved by a number of gold-framed – and very graphic depictions of various torture scenes. Also in the room was a pudgy man dressed in a black Basque, red suspenders and black stockings. He was standing with his back to them gyrating to the music.

Herbert cleared his throat loudly. "Er, scuse me squire!" he said loudly. The man turned around.

"Yes ducky," the man said as he reached over to turn off the music, "What can I do for you?" Henry did a double take.

"Hey don't I know you?"

"Could be ducky, I've been around...if you know what I mean."

"Obviously...you're down here." Henry said. Then the proverbial penny dropped. "Yes, you were behind me in the queue...Powder brackets Puff!"

"Ah, right. And you are Powder brackets Soap!"

"That's right," Henry replied. The other nodded "Small Hell!"

Henry returned the nod. "And you are

in charge of the Dungeons, or 'Donjons' as it says on the door... and you've only been down here for a short time!"

"Fast tracked," the man said. "Learnt a lot from working with one of Soho's top S&M madams..."

Herbert stepped forward.

"Sorry to interrupt an old pals' reunion here squire; but we are on official business..."

"Ooo isn't he the butch one then!" The Madonna fan said reaching forward and patting Herbert's arm.

"Here!" Herbert said taking a quick step backwards.

"Perhaps I can explain," Henry interrupted. "It's the laundry problem...we've come to try sort it out." The man squealed with delight.

"Oh you little love's! And not a day too soon look at the frills on me Basque. They've gone all limp and I can't do a thing with them!"

"Don't worry, we'll soon put some bounce back in them for you," Henry said pleasantly.

"Cheeky!"

Herbert interrupted again. "Your water works..."

"Of course, cheeky!"

"No, your plumbing..."

"Oooo!" Now Henry stepped forward.

"What our associate is trying to say is that there appears to be a fault in the mains water supply and we need to check all the, er, valves."

"Oh, how very blasé. Anyway how about a little drinky-poo before you get down to work? Gets pretty boring down here on my own."

"Drink?" Herbert said. "Well that's very neighbourly of you, er?"

"Gertie...You can leave the rude part out big boy!" Herbert smiled thinly.

"I'm Herbert and my associates are Henry and Wanda."

Introductions complete, Gertie sashayed over to the cabinet to collect a tray, glasses and a full bottle of liquor.

"Take a seat," he said nodding towards the black leather chesterfield, before placing the tray on the coffee table and sitting on the arm chair.

"Well this is cosy isn't it?" Gertie said. His guests, who had been glancing at the array of interesting art work smiled smiles that were decidedly thin.

Gertie reached out and picked up the bottle of liquor unscrewed the top and poured out generous measures into the four glasses. "*Satan's Sin* single malt whiskey, eighty four years matured." He said as he placed the bottle back down on the table and picked up one of the glasses.

"Chin chin!" he sang brightly, as with little finger bent he took a genteel sip. The guests picked up their glasses and followed suit (minus the little finger).

"Wow!" Herbert said in appreciation. "That really hits the spot; but do you think I could have a wee drop of water to go with it?"

"Off course ducky. Be back in two shakes of a demon's tail," Gertie said as he heaved himself to his feet and left the room.

As soon as he was gone Herbert reached into his boiler suit and withdrew the small bottle of pills. He unscrewed the top, popped one of the pills into their host's glass and then for good measure added another just to make sure. He then used a forefinger to quickly stir the contents.

He was halfway towards licking his finger, when he stopped. "Oops," he whispered. "Not a good idea!"

Gertie reappeared with the water and handed it over to Herbert, who smiled. "Thanks," Herbert said tipping the water into his drink and with a "Your health!" drained the glass. Gertie picked up his own glass and wished his guests a "Pleasant death!" Twenty seconds later he was a rag doll sprawled out on the carpet with one leg folded under him and a soppy grin on his face.

"Right," Herbert said, "He'll be in the land of nod for a good half hour; let's see what we can find."

Wanda spotted a large ring of keys hanging from a hook on one wall.

"Looks like those could be for the dungeons," she said. Herbert nodded, strode over and took the keys from their hook.

"Right," he muttered. "You two keep an eye on Gertie, while I go and investigate." Wanda turned to Henry.

"Shouldn't we go with him?" Henry considered it for a second.

"Safety in numbers and all that?" he said. Wanda nodded.

Henry then shook his head. "We're in the dungeons of Hell. Don't think three of us together would make much difference if everything suddenly went breasts up!"

Wanda considered the statement then shrugged. "Okay, give me a hand then to drag Gertie onto the sofa where he'll be more comfortable."

Henry reached down and heaved Gertie into an almost sitting position while Wanda grabbed the unconscious man's legs.

"Okay, on the count of three. One... Two... Three!" She said. Henry groaned as he grappled with the heavy end. He heaved and managed to manhandle Gertie onto the chesterfield and in the process managed to fall on top of him. One of Gertie's arms flopped over Henry's shoulder and the drugged man slurred: "Chheeeky."

***

Herbert moved through the kitchen area to another door that revealed a flight of stone steps, at the foot of which a gloomy passage beckoned. He took a deep breath and peering intently into the half light, made his way down.

The passage, which seemed to stretch into infinity was lined with dozens of heavy steel doors, each with a keyhole and a narrow twelve inch long slot at eye level. Herbert groaned, took a deep breath, approached the first one and peered through the slot into the black interior.

"Cobblers!" he mouthed.

"And fucking cobblers to you!" someone snarled. Herbert moved on to the next cell and repeated the first half of the secret code.

"Cobblers!" And he was told in no uncertain terms to go away and to perform an anatomically impossible sexual act upon himself. He sighed.

The next dozen or so cells offered up variations on the opening themes. He shook his head and muttered, "You'd think a lengthy stay in a cell would sharpen the mind to come up with something more original."

He approached the next cell and sighed almost in resignation.

"Cobblers," he said (without the exclamation mark). There was silence for a few heartbeats and then a quick whispered exchange between what sounded like, two people.

"Awls!" one of them shouted.

"I hear you guv'ner!" Herbert said as he fumbled with the ring of keys.

***

Back upstairs Henry and Wanda jumped with alarm as the kitchen door slammed back on its hinges and three men burst into the room.

Henry, seeing Ernie said, "Ernie! What are you doing here? We left you up top!"

"Tell him Ernie," Herbert said. Ernie nodded.

"I've been down there in a cell with Cyril here," he nodded towards the stranger, "for two months..." Henry frowned and shook his head.

"Two months? We only left you in your lift a short while ago!"

"That wasn't me," Ernie said flatly. "That was my identical twin, Bernie. He helped kidnap me when I was making a trip to Purgatory and took my place as liftman. He's been reporting back to Him ever since."

"But why?" Henry asked. Ernie shrugged.

"He was always the rebellious one. I suppose Big Nick buttered him up with promises of a big promotion or something." Henry nodded and then turned to the stranger.

"So you are the agent we came to find and hopefully rescue, Cyril?"

"That's me," the man said. "And mighty glad I am to make your acquaintance. For a while there I thought my goose was well cooked."

"Well, Herbert said, "I think..." Suddenly he stopped and bolted towards the front door which was slightly open.

"Gotcha!" they heard him shout in triumph, before he came back in, dragging 'Ernie' by the collar!

"Ernie...Bernie?" Henry exclaimed.

"The very same!" Herbert said. "I saw a hand edging around the door frame...I bet the little toe rag has been tailing us all along!"

"Yes I have," Bernie said calmly. "And just wait till I tell Big Nick what you lot are up to!" Herbert smiled lightly.

"Oh yes? And what do you think Big Nick will do to you when he gets to know of your balls up?" Bernie shook his head.

"What balls up? It wasn't me who got myself drugged and lost the keys. It's Gertie who will kop the shit, not me!" Herbert smiled thinly.

"Leaving that aside for a minute, you've been following us from the start right?"

"So?"

"So you've had plenty of time to turn us in along the way." Bernie shrugged.

"Now I wonder why you didn't do that? Was it because you wanted to play the super sleuth maybe?"

Bernie shrugged again, but this time there was a little hesitation before the shrug.

"So," Herbert continued, "when Big Nick hears we got away with the two prisoners... when you could easily have had us nabbed... what do you think his reaction might be? Well, I reckon he doesn't have a forgiving bone in his body so, if you were *very* lucky, he'd have you skinned alive and then when you recovered he'd have you skinned alive again every day for the next five hundred years...

"So, bit of a dilemma for you hey? We can lock you in one of the cells and leave you to Gertie's tender mercies – and when he reads the note we leave that tells him of your move to place the blame on him; well he won't be in a very forgiving mood will he?

"He has landed himself a cushy number down here and I think if I was him I would do anything to hang onto it.

"I reckon his best bet would be to leave you in one of the cells and forget about you for, say, a couple of hundred years or so..." Bernie swallowed nervously again.

"And if that doesn't worry you," Herbert continued, "and you still think you can come out of it smelling of roses, you can take your chances with Big Nick's notoriously fickle temper; which, I have to say, would be a remarkably bold decision on your part.

"Or... alternatively, you can come back with us and play the *mea culpa* card with the Boss's Son, who *does* have a very forgiving nature..." Bernie ran his tongue over suddenly dry lips.

"And what would He do to me then?"

"I reckon He would give you fifty years or so in Purgatory... which would be a Hell of a lot better than getting yourself skinned alive every day for the next five hundred years..." Bernie looked down at the floor for several long seconds then nodding slowly, he looked back up.

"Okay," he said simply.

"You know it makes sense," Herbert said brightly.

Chapter 13

Jesus shook His head, sighed and lifting up
the golf bag, slipped the strap over a
shoulder. He wasn't in the best of moods.
And the attire He was wearing did nothing to
lighten that mood either.

"Plus fours, a Paisley pattern sweater,
Argyle socks and a bloody oversized *tam 'o
shanter* hat," He said to the mirror, before
moving on from His wardrobe, He glanced
for the hundredth time in the last few days at
the monstrosity perched on the end of His
nose.

He sighed again then thought *If He has
a good round and whups Lucy's arse, maybe He'll
be in a good enough mood to rid me of the bloody
thing.* Then He thought of when Joan had
come back into the office after her emergency
visit to the hairdressers with her new ultra
cropped hairstyle and *He* had said in a voice
that dripped with the honey of innocence, but
behind which lurked the acid of revenge:

"So who's the new little dyke then?"

*Maybe I should stay as close to Him as I
can and that will at least give me a chance to jump
in if I see any sign of a relapse*, He thought.

He took a final look in the mirror at

His ensemble... and sighed again.

It was bad enough his Pater had become a golf nut, but why could He not have adopted a less ridiculous mode of dress! "I'm going to look a right prawn," He muttered. "While Lucy and his caddie will probably turn up looking like something straight out of the pages of Vogue magazine; if they have a men's section in Vogue magazine of course." He sighed again and then thought *I'm doing a lot of bloody sighing lately.*

The thought almost made Him sigh again; but He squared His shoulders, rapped on his Dad's door and was almost immediately bid enter.

"You look the part Son," God said admiringly as He checked out His Son's snazzy ensemble; which was, as it happened identical to His own. Jesus managed a weak smile, while thinking *Tweedle Dee and bloody Tweedle Dum.*

"Right Pater," He said... and then with an effort to suppress another sigh, "Click Your fingers and teleport Us to the links."

In the twinkling of an eye they were stood outside the first tee where God said "Driver Son, while I loosen up a bit before *he* gets here."

Back at head office there was a flash of light accompanied by a definite whiff of brimstone in the air that caused Joan, who was sitting at her desk, to jump in alarm as a snappily dressed Lucifer and his little imp caddie materialised in front of her.

"I do wish you would not do that!" she complained. Lucifer smiled.

"Apologies dear lady," he said smoothly, while slowly arching an eyebrow that somehow managed to suggest that there was a history of sexual chemistry between them.

Joan rose to her feet and nodded slowly towards the tall, tanned, blue eyed, black curly haired Adonis: while thinking *Oh my! He is a handsome devil... even if I know that's not his true likeness."*

Seconds later her knees went all a tremble as he strode forward, lifted her limp hand and kissed it tenderly. She blushed, pulled away (slowly) and managed to plonk herself back down on her chair.

"Wow! You nearly got her goin' there Boss. Bet you could bend her over the desk and slip her one right now!" his caddy leered.

Joan gasped. Lucifer shook his head slowly.

"Would you excuse me a moment dear lady," he said. She nodded dumbly. He turned.

"Please hand me the five iron Midjee." The imp reached up into the bag, withdrew a club and handed it over. Lucifer seemed to study it for a second or two, before twisting it round so that the blunt heel was facing directly downwards... and rapped his caddy smartly, CLUNK... Bang between his little horns.

"OW! Fuck Boss, that fuckin' hurt!" This statement brought an immediate second rap. CLUNK... "OW! Fuck...Fuck!" Lucifer shook his head and tutted.

"Now then," he said tiredly. "I am going to do it again. But before I do I want you to know why."

Midjee rubbed the second lump that, alongside the first now gave him the appearance of being the possessor of a second pair of embryonic horns. He grimaced then nodded slowly.

"It is because we are in the presence of a lady, not one of the succubi trollops from back home...you understand?" Midjee nodded.

"And when I do deliver the reprimand, you will not respond with foul language, understand?" the imp nodded and screwed his little red eyes tightly shut.

CLUNK "OW! FFFFFFFFFF!"

"Right, lesson delivered; but learned? I somehow doubt it," he said turning to Joan and shrugging lightly. He then smiled, arched an eyebrow again and said,

"Anyway, a pleasure as always to see you my dear; but I fear we are running a little late, so we must away now." Joan nodded. There was a second flash of light and then just before the visitors winked out of existence, she was almost sure that she saw Midjee cup his claws over where his crotch would be (if he had one) and make an extremely crude gesture in her direction.

***

"He's here," Jesus said, nodding towards a spot ten yards to their left. "And he's got that obnoxious little imp, Midjee, with him again. And, yes, just as I thought they're dressed like something out of a flashy men's magazine. Matching Armani suits, slightly off-white, white Ralph Lauren cashmere roll neck sweaters and hand stitched Italian crocodile shoes.... if I am not mistaken."

He adjusted his floppy *tam o' shanter* and sighed again.

"Alright Lucy, how's it hanging?" God said as the newcomers approached. Lucifer managed a thin smile.

"Fine, just fine, and you?"

"Oh, you know, not bad, apart from the odd twinge." Lucifer held his hand out to Jesus who was stood nearest to him.

"And how are you Jaycee?" He said brightly, flashing a mouthful of dazzlingly white, perfectly shaped teeth. Jesus' eyes narrowed slightly. The last time they had met Lucifer had had one of those little electric shock buzzer things hidden in his palm.

"Oh," Lucifer said noticing a slight reluctance as a hand was held out towards him. "No tricks this time Jaycee!" They shook, after which Lucifer said "Wow that's some bugle you've got there Jaycee, looks like the red and purple arse end of a baboon..."

Jesus bit His lip and took a deep breath.

Don't sink to his level, He thought. *Rise above it and that will show him that you are a superior being who does not resort to cheap jibes about another's looks.*

"Smart threads," Jesus replied, nodding towards Lucifer's suit. "Apart from the sweaters that look a little off colour, if you don't mind Me saying..." Lucifer pulled a wry face.

"Laundry problem. Your Dad has kindly sent an expert down to see if he can sort it out."

"Oh really," Jesus said in what was a fair stab at a surprised voice. "Let's hope he can do that then; you do have a reputation to maintain after all."

Introductions over God placed a ball on a tee, addressed it, and took a couple of practice swings. Nodding slightly He drew his arm back and swung... just as Midjee coughed loudly. The ball skipped forward about six feet. There was a sudden and not very distant rumble of thunder as God glared at the imp, who shrugged and innocently pointed to his throat.

Lucifer tutted. "Midjee," he said tiredly, "Five iron please." The imp grimaced.

"Er, permission to swear Boss?" He said.

"Permission granted."
Swing...CLUNK... "OWWW! FUCK!"

Chapter 14

Herbert led with Ernie and Bernie behind him followed by Henry, Wanda, and Cyril bringing up the rear. They had only been on their way for a minute or two, when Cyril moved up to Henry's shoulder and whispered "Hang back a pace or two." Henry glanced across at Wanda, who shrugged lightly. "Go on," she said softly.

When he had done as asked Henry whispered "What's so secret that the others can't hear?"

"Not the others; Bernie. I don't want him to hear. We can't trust him yet."

"Hear what?" Cyril looked ahead to make sure that they would be out of earshot.

"It's about my orders to find out what Big Nick is planning."

"And, did you find out anything?"

"Yes, but that's the problem..." Henry frowned.

"Problem?"

"Yes. The problem is I don't think it is Big Nick who is planning something." Henry almost skidded to a stop.

"So, he is not... But someone else is!"

"Yes."

"Who?"

"That's just it! I'm not sure; but it is almost certainly at least one of the Princes..." Henry frowned.

"Princes; what Princes?"

"One of Hell's Princes...You not been dead long then?" he said.

"No, but it's beginning to feel like a hundred years."

"Oh right. Anyway, just before I got rumbled I got wind of a secret meeting of Princes coming up."

"Secret? So you mean secret even from Big Nick?" Cyril nodded. "Secret especially from Big Nick."

"Why, surely he is the head honcho down here?"

"Of course, he is very much the Prime Prince of Hell, while the others, Beelzebub, Mammon, Leviathan, Asmodeus , Belphegor and Amon are his subordinates. And it is they who I am talking about."

"But why does it look like they are plotting something?"

"Not sure, but I reckon there is a feeling afoot that he is going soft..."

"Soft! You call roasting people on spits or skinning them alive, is going soft!"

"No, not that; he keeps up with tradition on that score. It's his relationship with the The Big Man."

"You mean GOD?"

"Yes; you know that he was once one of the Big Man's favourites don't you?"

"Well yes, I do remember something from bible studies a long time ago..."

"Well it seems they are even golfing buddies nowadays..."

"My word!"

"My word is right!"

"But how can they be buddies! The whole concept of Good and Bad, Heaven and Hell, is based on them being deadly adversaries!"

"Well yeah they are really, but by the looks of this golfing thing that's what has got the Princes on edge, there seems to be a slight thawing in their relationship."

"And why do you think that has come about then?" Cyril scratched his head.

"Can't say really; but I think maybe the Big Man is a bit sorry for Lucifer; oh and by the way do you know what the name Lucifer translates as in ancient Aramaic?"

"Believe it or not, no I don't know what the name translates as in ancient Aramaic," Henry said shaking his head slowly.

"It means 'Son of the Morning'; bit ironic that don't you think bearing in mind his current nature and abode?"

"Well yes I guess it does; but anyway

what's the bit about God feeling sorry for him?"

"Look, when the Gaffer created man He gave him/her Free Will yes?"

"Yes, so?"

"Well when he created the angels he didn't give them Free Will..."

"Which means?"

"Which means that...unlike man's Free Will that allowed him the freedom of choice – and what a balls up he has made of that – they couldn't rebel against His Will. So for Lucifer and his crew to do just that they had to be like hard wired to rebel." Henry, who had never really taken any interest in matters theological, nodded slowly.

"So really Lucifer didn't have a choice, is that what you're saying?"

"Correctamundo."

"Okay, I get that; but what about God feeling sorry for Lucifer?"

"I suppose that over the millennia He has had time to ponder on that and maybe He now feels that Lucifer was dealt a bum hand before the game even started..."

"Right so if what you are saying is true and there is a thawing in their relationship, that is going to impact on Hell and that is what these Princes are pissed off about."

"Yeah. For thousands of years each one has been *Numero Uno* in his particular

Sector of Hell and none of them wants to run the risk of losing any power." Henry nodded.

"So who else knows about the possible plot that these Princes could be putting together?"

"Well, just me and you now."

"You didn't discuss it with Ernie in the cell then?" Cyril shook his head.

"No I thought it best to keep it to myself until, hopefully, I got free."

"Didn't they try torture on you then in order to find out what you were up to?"

"Oh yes, they did that alright..."

"What thumb screws and such..."

"No, bit more drastic than that."

"What like?" Cyril shrugged.

"Oh, they ripped out my liver a few times and barbecued it in front of me for the imps to snack on." Henry's mouth flapped open.

"OH...MY...GOD!" he gasped. Cyril just shrugged.

"They gave up after a while and just bunged me in a cell." Henry shook his head slowly and shivered. Cyril noticed his reaction.

"Look," he said calmly. "It did hurt like bloody hell; but if anything, the mental trauma was even worse than the physical which actually healed itself within a couple of days. I guess though that if there is any lasting effect it probably centres around my definite distaste for offal on a dinner plate!"

"Enough to turn anybody vegetarian I should think," Henry said, with another little shiver.

They walked on together for another minute before Henry said: "So what are you going to do now other than tell the Boss about your suspicions...and let's face it; that's all they are now, just suspicions, right?" Cyril nodded slowly.

"I reckon we will have to get someone on the inside who can sniff around in the Sectors that the other Princes rule. I've been rumbled so my cover is well and truly blown." Henry nodded slowly then said gloomily:

"Yes, so I wouldn't mind betting that my reputation as the world's leading soap powder expert will be getting a wider airing in the not too distant future..."

Chapter 15

"Well played," Lucifer said holding out a hand to God, who took it and said,

"Well I was a little lucky." *Yes you were,* Lucifer thought. *Especially on the fifteenth and sixteenth when your drives landed at least twenty yards from the hole; but by the time we got near the pin those twenty yards had suddenly and miraculously shrunk to no more three.*

"No, not at all," Lucifer replied. "Your game today was just a little too strong for me I'm afraid. You must have been working out lately because you seem to have added at least twenty yards to your drives..." God shrugged.

"Just practice and more practice, Lucy. They do say it makes perfect. And anyway you almost got me this time with those two remarkable holes in one on twelve and fourteen!" *Remarkable,* He thought, *when We thought your drives might have ended up in the rough, but lo and behold, when Midjee ran ahead, he found that the balls were in fact nestling in the cup!*

"Well, I have also been *practicing,*" Lucifer said lightly. God nodded.

"Well it was a good close game and the

drinks are on Me Lucy if you would like to adjourn to the Clubhouse."

"Most kind," Lucifer said. "But I have a busy schedule, so if you will excuse me, I will say *adieu* until our next game." God nodded.

"Look forward to it and I bet you can't repeat those remarkable *hole in one* feats next time!" Lucifer smiled.

"And I bet you won't be able to outdrive me again next time either!" Lucifer replied as he signalled Midjee to his side and made ready to snap his fingers for the return journey to Hell.

He raised his hand and put his thumb and third finger together, but just before he made the move he turned to Jesus and said "Hope you've got rid of that baboon's arse on the end of Your nose before we meet again Jaycee."

***

Back at Head Office the telephone in Joan's office rang. "Cyril!" she said, then "No, they are not here, they are on the golf course...Yes the Boss is playing Lucifer...Oh about another couple of hours I should think...Yes, right, ring back; okay, speak later. Oh, and nice to finally have you back safe and sound!"

Cyril made his way back to the table in *The Angel* where the others - apart from Bernie - were relaxing. He was nervously biting on his bottom lip.

"They are on the golf course with your ex Boss," Cyril said casually. "So you might as well try and unwind over the next couple of hours."

"Easy for you to say," Bernie muttered. Cyril nodded.

"Maybe, but look at it this way; whatever comes your way is going to be a whole lot more pleasant than what would have been coming if you hadn't seen the light."

"What fifty years of so in Purgatory, you mean?"

"Yeah, do that on your head, I should think...and it might not even be that much of a stretch. I'll put in a good word...tell the Boss that you are a serious Repenter...unless your Ernie thinks I shouldn't of course..." Bernie looked across the table at Ernie and then swallowed nervously.

"Yeah... Well..." Ernie said slowly. Bernie swallowed again. "I suppose blood is thicker and all that..." Bernie let out a breath he was holding.

"Thanks our kid," he said, then added "What's everyone having; it's my shout!"

As Bernie made his way over to the bar

Cyril cleared his throat loudly. "While he's at the bar I can tell you that the rest of us will soon be meeting up with the Boss and His Son." Henry's eyes opened wider.

"Actual GOD and JESUS!" he said.

"Shhh!" Cyril replied.

"Sorry..." Henry apologised, glancing around the room. "But THE actual God and Jesus..." he said, before adding a whispered "Wow."

"But before I spoke to Head Office," Cyril said. "I gave the Chief of Security, 'Nosy' Parker a bell and he will be here in a few minutes to take us to a de-briefing. He will also have a member of his team with him, who will conduct Bernie to a waiting cell, before he is interrogated." Everyone around the table nodded slowly.

Bernie returned carrying a tray of drinks which they hardly had time to take a couple of sips from, before Parker and an assistant turned up.

"Cyril," the security chief said tilting up his sunglasses to make sure he was talking to the right person. "Nice to see you back. Hope things weren't too hairy for you down there." Cyril shook his head.

"Not really boss, apart from a bit of liver trouble."

"Good man. And you Ernie, you okay too?"

"Yes sir, I am now I'm back home."

'Nosy' then turned to Bernie and frowned.

"And you my lad; got yourself in deep doo doo eh?" Bernie bowed his head.

"Yes sir, but thankfully I saw the error of my ways..."

"Yes well, let's hope it's the Boss' Son who will deal with that and not the Boss Himself. He can be particularly Old Testament Tough at the minute; while His Son is very much the forgiving One in the family."

Bernie nodded gloomily. "Anyway," Parker continued. "You toddle off with my associate lad, while I take everyone else for a thorough debriefing...and leave those drinks behind," he ordered. "The coming home party just got wound up early."

Chapter 16

"Well," Henry said stifling a yawn. "Four hours debriefing, that certainly was thorough!"

"And it's not over yet," Herbert said, looking around the table and nodding at Wanda and Ernie. "Nosy and Cyril will have to collate all the info and get it down on disc for the Boss and His Son to go over and then we'll all have to go over to Head Office and answer any questions that they want answering."

"Great!" Henry said. "I can't wait to see The Actual GOD...and of course Jesus! What do they look like? Does God have a long white beard and dress in a long white robe; and does Jesus look like he does on all those crosses you see in churches, like pale and wounded looking?" Herbert shook his head.

"No not really; all those paintings and what not are hundreds of years old. Though physically, The Boss probably does look quite a bit like that painting on the *Sistine Chapel* ceiling, you know the one where He is lay back and touching forefingers with Adam

who is lay back opposite. In that one The
Boss is looking pretty muscular and potent
like, with kind of thick dark wavy head and
beard hair that is turning to iron grey."

"And Jesus, what about Him?"

"Well, He probably looks a bit like
your typical sixties hippy I suppose. Not
spaced out of course! And not like, 'hey
man' and all that hippie crapspeak; but
y'know like 'intense' like."

"I can't wait!" Henry said.

"Well, while you can't wait, how about
getting another round in then?" Herbert said
nodding towards the bar.

An hour later a loud snatch of harp
music, played over the pub speaker system to
signal last orders.

"Don't know about you people,"
Henry said. "But it's been a long day for me.
I think I need to get away to me bed."

"I think that's a good idea," Herbert
said. Wanda and Ernie were quick to nod in
agreement.

Outside, Herbert and Ernie said their
goodnights to Henry and Wanda and they all
agreed to meet for a pub lunch the next day
at one o'clock.

"Well then Wanda I'll walk you to
your flat," Herbert said stifling another yawn.
Wanda smiled.

"Are you really that tired then Henry?"

"Yes, I'm as they say, 'cream crackered'."

"Are- you- really- that- tired- then-Henry?" she repeated slowly.

"Oh, right...maybe not quite..."

***

The little party of six, headed up by Parker, filed into Head Office Reception, where Joan slid out from her chair and moved to greet them.

"Welcome," she said warmly. "They are waiting for you in the Boss' office, I'll just bell them." She reached over for the telephone .

"They are here Sir, shall I send them through?"

"Yes send them through," a deep well modulated voice said in answer. The hairs on the back of Henry's neck did a little dance. *Wow* he thought, *THE Actual GOD and I am about to meet Him!*

Joan opened the door and stood back as they filed in.

The two men; one appeared to be in his early sixties, the other early to mid thirties, were sat behind a large dark mahogany desk. The younger man, who had dark brown hair almost falling onto his shoulders, rose to his feet and approached the newcomers ... and Henry gaped.... He was wearing a pair of faded blue denim bootcut jeans with frayed knees and a pair of three inch heeled, dark brown cowboy boots. He also wore a rainbow patterned tee shirt that had a white centre panel with the words *Jesus is Cool!* printed across the chest.

"Welcome," the man said softly. "Please pull up seats and we'll get down to business." He indicated a row of chairs that were lined up against a back wall, and thirty seconds later the six were ranged around the desk.

Five of them looked as though this was a run of the mill situation; the sixth sat there with his mouth hanging half open, looking across the desk at the older man who was wearing a green and brown camouflage tee shirt tucked into dark green cargo trousers. Henry could not see His feet, but he was pretty sure they would be encased in a pair of combat boots, or failing that, Doc Martins.

"Now then," Jesus said, "Dad and I have studied your comprehensive report... and congratulations on that," He added, nodding towards them.

Five of them smiled lightly; the sixth still had his mouth hanging half open.

"And from that report it would seem that Lucifer is perhaps not complicit in any possible devilry that might be afoot." The Boss nodded slowly.

"Yes," He said in a bass voice. "It looks as though I might have jumped to the wrong conclusions where Lucy was concerned and If so I might have to apologise when I see him."

"And that," Jesus said, "will be in about another hour, as Dad spoke to him on the hot line earlier and requested a meeting here in our office."

"Excuse me Sir," 'Nosy' Parker said nodding towards The Boss. "But did you mention anything on the blower about our suspicions?" God shook his head.

"I might be getting on a wee bit in years my boy, but I am far from in my dotage!" Nosy squirmed lightly.

"No of course not Boss! I just wanted to check... Part of my brief as Head of Security and all that..." God nodded, but favoured His Security Head with a long steely stare.

Henry - who had by now closed his mouth, noticed the stare and thought *Bloody Hell, I wouldn't want to get on the wrong side of The Big Man!* The Big Man then seemed to glance directly at Henry for a second causing him to mentally add: *Oh my G...Can He read minds!* Then: *Of course He can if He has a mind to...He is God after all!* He risked making eye contact that he did not really want to make, thinking: *What if He did read my mind! And me calling Him the Big Man! Oh G... Will He be offended by my lack of respect!*

Fortunately, God's glance had been just that, and now He was passing His eyes along the seated line... before speaking again.

"I said a little earlier that I might have to apologise to Lucy. That depends on whether We decide to take him fully into Our confidence. By that I mean do We tell him about the possible threat posed by the other Princes of Hell; or do We keep Our suspicions to Ourselves, sit back and enjoy the carnage that could result?

"Some," He glanced at Jesus, "are of the opinion that he is the Devil Incarnate and We should not have any dealings with him that could result in a possible interruption to the present *status quo*. He is the Baddie and We are the Goodies...to use a hackneyed cowboy term," He added, glancing down at Jesus' boots.

"But if We *don't* take him into Our confidence there is the possibility that caught unawares, he could, even with his superior power, be overthrown and replaced by 'X' the Unknown."

The six nodded slowly. "Is it not best that We stick with the Devil We know?" He looked each of them in the eye and after a

few moments all six nodded firmly. "Good,"
He said simply, "That's what I had decided
anyway."

"So," Jesus said, "As the decision has
already been taken," He glanced across at
God. "There will probably be a further role
for some of you, depending on Lucifer's
reaction to the news that there is a possible
coup on the horizon.

"He may choose to ignore Our
warnings, thinking either that We are trying
to stir up trouble down there; or failing that
and he believes Our warning, he could ignore
it, confident that he is powerful enough to
slap down any embryonic rebellion."

Herbert put his hand up. "Excuse me
Sir; You mentioned a possible further role for
some of us. Can You expand on that please?"

"Well, if Lucy does accept Our news of
a possible rebellion and he doesn't want to
risk going off half cocked, so to say, without
firm proof of any skulduggery, he very well
might want Heaven to help out with the
detective work. In which case, Cyril and
Ernie, who are both Hell's absconding
'guests' should not be included, as they might
arouse suspicion; as would Mr Parker, who is
known in his capacity as Head of Security.

"Henry and Herbert, on the other
hand have already been given access to tackle
the source of the laundry problem. They

would be free to visit the other levels that are the domain of the Princes; where they might pick up useful information that could turn Our suspicions into hard fact."

"Er, excuse me Sir," Henry said. "But what about Wanda?" Jesus frowned lightly.

"Yes; what about Wanda?" Henry cleared his throat.

"Well Sir, we did form a team and it strikes me that two men ferreting around are more likely to rouse suspicion than a little delegation that includes a woman...and I don't mean that in a sexist way!" He added, with a quick glance in Wanda's direction.

Jesus nodded slowly and then turned to God, who, after a few seconds, returned the nod.

"Very well," Jesus said. "You may reform your 'team' if Lucifer agrees that Our help is needed. In the meantime I call this meeting to a close and you all better high tail it out of here ... before you run into the *Arch Fiend* on his way in."

God glanced down at His Son's cowboy boots again, sighed lightly and shook His head ultra slowly.

Chapter 17

"Good afternoon dear lady," Lucifer said smoothly as he blinked into existence three feet in front of the seated Joan... who jumped again.

"Oops sorry dear lady, I really must see if I can rig up a little chime that announces me before I materialise."

Joan smiled weakly, while *thinking Oh my, I'm glad I am sitting this time and he won't see me go weak at the knees!*

"Well, that would be most considerate," she said, trying not to look into his gorgeous cobalt blue eyes. He nodded.

"And talking of 'consideration' you can see that for the sake of decorum and to save any maidenly blushes, I have not brought a certain uncouth little imp with me this time."

As the embarrassing memory played back every excruciating second in her head, Joan did blush, but Lucifer, in rare gallantly mode, pretended not to notice; instead he said. "Are they waiting for me in the office dear lady?" Joan nodded dumbly before clearing her throat and finding her voice.

"Yes they are sir I will announce your

arrival."

Inside the office Lucifer strode over to the desk and nodded at Jesus.

"Ah, I see that baboon's arse on the end of your nose has gone JayCee," he said.

Jesus took a slow breath, smiled thinly, but did not reply. Lucifer then turned towards God.

"He must have apologised for whatever it was that caused that abomination then?" God waved a hand in dismissal.

"Not important Lucy," He said. "But something else is; and that is why We have asked you to come back so soon after your last visit."

"I'm all ears... rather than all nose," Lucifer said winking at Jesus.

"We think that the other Princes of Hell may be in the process of organising a coup against you Lucy," God said bluntly. Lucifer blinked and then laughed.

"A coup! I don't think so! None of them would have the balls!"

"That's not Our impression..."

"Then what is your impression...and how did you come by it?"

"We had an agent on site..." Lucifer bristled.

"An agent! We had an agreement that neither of us would interfere in the other's business!" God shook his head.

"An agreement that you also ignored when you kidnapped one of our people, a lift operator, and replaced him with his identical twin brother who you had seduced into your service." Lucifer blinked again.

"How did..." God held up a hand.

"You know Lucy, you've been spending too much time down on earth spreading shit lately and your minions don't seem to be up to your standard.

"We rescued our agent, also our kidnapped lift operator and the turncoat twin, who has now returned to our fold."

"Oh right...Anyway I am expected to be devious and cunning, I am the Prince of Darkness after all; while you lot are all supposed to be whiter than white and holier than I!" God shook His head.

"Listen Lucy, there's no point in arguing the toss. Our agent got a whiff of a plot before one of your second rate demons had him thrown into the pokey and tortured; unsuccessfully I might add.

"We rescued him and that is why you are standing here."

"And why are you telling me all this when you could just sit back and watch the fun?"

"Because it is better to stick with the devil you know, rather than a cabal of loose Canons, who could cause mayhem for everyone concerned.

"We have obviously had plenty of differences in the past, but in the last few centuries tensions have eased off a tad...and We think maybe that has a bearing on this coup thing." Lucifer stroked his chin.

"So, are you saying that our decision to treat each other with some kind of tolerance and respect has led to the Princes suspecting a softening in both our characters?" God nodded.

"There are our golf dates and of course the invitation for you and your senior staff to enjoy the odd change of scenery up here..."

"Yes, I suppose that might get up some of their noses. Might make some of them a little wary of me going soft..."

"Precisely," God said. "So what are you going to do about the situation?"

"What I should do is round the bastards up, find out who the ringleader is and turn him into a pot plant for my patio; that's what I should do."

"Yes, an understandable course of action I am sure," God said blithely. "But as I have already said, there isn't any hard evidence to hand."

"Then We have to get some." God nodded.

"And are you saying with the 'We' that you want Our assistance in this matter?"

Lucifer thought it over for ten seconds before nodding firmly.

***

"It's' on!" Herbert said the next afternoon in *The Angel*.

"The boss just rang me on the hot line at my turnstile half an hour ago and told me that Old Nick wants our help in tracking down the culprits!" Henry swallowed nervously.

"Oh right," he said with what appeared to be a distinct lack of enthusiasm.

"What, you not up for it then?"

"Well, I'm not really the cloak and dagger sort..."

"Bollocks! You've done okay so far haven't you?" Henry managed to transmit an 'I don't really know about that', into a shrug.

"Course you have," Herbert said brightly; "an' anyway we're a team aren't we, you, me and Wanda?"

"Well, yes, I suppose so..."

"Well then...it will be an adventure!"

And those last five words dragged Henry's mind back to the last time he had heard them; when they were uttered from his own mouth on an Austrian nursery slope. And more to the point the memory dragged his mind back to the consequences that soon followed their utterance...namely his death.

"Won't it?" Herbert said.

"What?"

"Be a big adventure! Were you away with the fairies or something then?"

"Well, I was on an Austrian *piste,* actually; but that was a hundred years ago..." Herbert shook his head.

"This *Harp* lager tastes like maid's piss to me, but I think maybe you should go on shandies my son." Henry was about to respond but stopped as he spotted Wanda coming through the door.

"Sorry I'm late," she said breezily as she took a seat at their table.

"Only a couple of minutes," Henry said nudging a glass of lime and soda over to her. She smiled.

"Thank you kind sir; and by the look on *your* face Herbert, you have some news to impart, yes?"

"It's green light and all stations go!" Henry sighed.

"What our companion is saying in a gung ho voice is that Lucifer has asked for Heaven's help and you, Herbert and I have the honour of being the first over the top into enemy territory..."

"Hey, neat!" Wanda said.

"Neat Wanda! It was bad enough going into one of Hell's strongholds; now we are strolling into five more!" Wanda shrugged.

"Well after spending the last ten years or so shuffling papers around down in Purgatory I would welcome some more adventure." Herbert nodded.

"That's what I just told him. It will be an adventure I said!" Henry held his arms up in surrender.

"Okay," he said. "It will be an adventure. Now Herbert, what's the plan?"

"We are to rendezvous with Nosy Parker tomorrow at oh nine hundred hours..." Henry sighed loudly. "Where," Herbert continued, "He will fill us in on each of the Princes character and how we should approach them. When we get down below again I of course will use my plumbing expertise to blind them with science, while you can do the same regarding soapy things..."

"Soapy things..." Henry said, adding another loud sigh. "And Wanda, what is she to be an expert in?"

"As a Grade Two Liaison Officer, she will be our superior, so she is the one who will field any questions thrown at us about what we are doing down there."

"Grade Two!" Wanda said. "Why can't I be Grade One?" Henry sighed again.

Chapter 18

After a rerun of basic counter intelligence and surveillance techniques for the benefit of Wanda, Nosy Parker placed a flip chart on an easel and said "We will now go through a basic introduction of Hell's Princes and their natures, okay?" Henry, Herbert and Wanda nodded.

"Right," he said as he reached up and with a flamboyant gesture flicked over the cover to the first page, which was headed by the word **Lucifer**.

"Lucifer, or Lucy as The Boss frequently calls him to get up his nose is, as you can see from the bullet points, the undisputed (at the moment anyway) leader of all of Hells legions. All the other princes answer to him.

"He once had beauty, wisdom, ability, perfection: but he wanted more. He wanted to be worshipped like God. For that he was the first angel to be booted out of Heaven, due to the sin of Pride."

Nosy flipped to the next page which was headed by the name: **Beelzebub**

"Now, Beelzebub was the second of The Boss's angels to get the boot. He is sometimes referred to as '*Lord of the Flies*'. This is a perversion of his original Philistine name 'Baalzebub' which translates as '*Lord of All That Flies*'. It was the Hebrews who changed his name to Beelzebub: Lord of the Flies.

"His downfall was due to the sin of Gluttony and he is ranked Number Two in power behind Lucifer.

"The next page, is headed as you can see by the word **Leviathan**

"His sin was 'Envy' and his realm is mostly the sea; where he often appears in the form of a terrifying monster of the deep.

"The Book of Job devotes an entire chapter (*Job41*) to Leviathan, which gives you some idea of his importance; and indeed, he is an evil demonic spirit of Envy.

"Next we see that the page is headed by the word **Mammon**

"Mammon's downfall was due to the sin of Greed. He is known as the '*Lord of Avarice* and – he also has a well-earned reputation for duplicity."

"Next, we have **Belphagor**

"He could accurately be described as one big lazy bastard; as it was Sloth that got him kicked out. In his present form his role is to sow discord among humans and to seduce them to evil."

"Next, we come to **Amon**.

"He was a stroppy angel who was notoriously bad tempered and it was this that got him the boot for the sin of Wrath.

"In his present form he is in charge of creating hate and anger in the human heart.

"And finally we have a page headed by the word **Asmodeus**.

"Asmodeus is – excuse me here madam, for my indelicate language – a right horny bastard!" Wanda suddenly became Extra Attentive (with a capital 'A' and 'E').

"And he, as one might suspect, was an angel who fell prey to the sin of Lust, in all its seedy guises; so his *raison 'd'être'* is to twist human's sexual desires.

"These then are the Lords of Hell and each of them has dominion over legions of minor devils and imps; with Lucifer of course the supreme commander. Henry shook his head slowly.

"Phew!" He said. "I always thought of Hell as being just one big underworld of fire and brimstone, with Satan/Lucifer as the Tormentor in Chief. I didn't realise that he could have delegated to such an extent." Nosy smiled thinly.

"Lucy is, when all is said and done, only one Devil and I am sure it can't have escaped your notice, Mr Pratt, that with billions of people down on Earth there are a Hell of a lot of potential candidates for eternal damnation... and hence, the need for a more equitable doling out of the work load." Henry nodded.

"Right," Nosy said in a businesslike voice. "Do any of you have any questions regarding what you have just heard?" His audience exchanged quick glances before all three shook their heads.

"Good, so I will finish off with a few more tips regarding your target's characters, before you will be fitted with personal trackers which can be monitored from the main console at security HQ.

"I could also supply you with the latest Nokia mobile phones, but they would be quickly confiscated toot sweet upon your arrival. But even if they weren't confiscated, they wouldn't be much use, because reception down there is notoriously crap."

Henry nodded firmly; he looked on mobile phones as an abomination and had often daydreamed about the wailing and gnashing of teeth that would surely engulf at least half of the 'civilised' world's population if a few communications satellites should somehow mysteriously fall from the sky...

Parker wound up the briefing by highlighting some more of the princes' character traits before adding a note of caution.

"You may get the impression," he said sternly, "that some of them; Belphagor and Amon, for instance spring to mind, are perhaps not the sharpest utensils in the knife drawer. That might be true, but they are princes when all is said and done and what they may lack in brains they certainly compensate for in cunning and in their single minded determination to stay at the top of their particular tree.

"Underestimate them at your peril."

Henry shifted a little uncomfortably in his seat.

The briefing over, Parker took them from the briefing room to Security HQ's workshop area where they were each fitted with hidden micro trackers that were cunningly moulded into the plastic identification cards which were to be pinned to their chest at all times

"Obviously it is very much in your best interest to stay as close together as you can, thus reducing the risk of one of you becoming isolated. If however one of you should get isolated or worse, be taken for any reason, we will at least be able to track him or her, which will improve the chances of rescue. Everyone got that?" They all nodded firmly.

"Good. Now Herbert and Henry, before you set off we will need to temporarily remove your halos as we don't want to antagonise anyone down there. So, gentlemen, if you will step over to my associates, they will take care of that quickly."

Henry and Herbert did as requested and one of Parker's white lab coat wearing techs then entered data into a console, while the second man stood behind Henry and Herbert with a device that resembled a miniature metal detector. At a nod from the tech at the console he then raised the device above Henry's head. There was a loud beep and Henry's halo plopped down onto his crown. This was repeated with Herbert and within two minutes the now halo-less pair were back with Wanda and Parker.

"Feels a bit odd," Henry said as he waved a hand above his head. Parker nodded.

"You will get them back," he said, "when you complete your mission." Henry took a deep breath and thought *If we complete our mission don't you mean...*

Nosy then said "If you are challenged at any time your answer is that you have been seconded from Purgatory at the request of Lucifer who has learned of Henry's remarkable grasp of all things relating to laundering." He then pointed to the card pinned to Henry's boiler suit.

"As you will notice Lucifer's sigil appears on your ID cards and nobody will overrule it by denying you access to any area you choose to enter." Henry tilted the card and studied the strange amalgam of squiggles that sat at the bottom of the card.

"Sigil?" He said. Parker nodded.

"It is his signature for all intents and purposes. Each of the princes has his own personal sigil.

"And this," he said handing Wanda a slim two inch square piece of plastic resembling a credit card, "is your key to the SEL, the Super Express Lift. Without this key or one like it, nobody can get into the lift, let alone use it. So follow me...and first stop Prince Beelzebub, The Lord of the Flies..."

Chapter 19

This lift was different to the others that Henry had become intimately acquainted with recently. It looked sleeker, racier, static, yet somehow...poised for flight; or rather poised for heart in mouth 'plummet'.

"I suppose it goes rather fast?" Henry said looking at the cigar shaped stainless steel pod. Nosy nodded.

"Almost supersonic probably; so you will all need to be strapped in." Henry blew out his cheeks.

"Couldn't God have like, snapped His fingers or something instead and just transported us instantly that way?"

"Probably, but that would only have got you down to the first stopping off point wouldn't it?" Henry sighed.

"Yes, but it was a nice thought anyway."

"Plus," Parker said. "If He did that it would look like He was actively breaching His agreement with Lucifer by interfering directly." Henry sighed again.

"Right," he said in weary resignation, "let's get strapped in then."

The pod announced their arrival with a 'ding' and the words "Sector 1, Level 100, Lord Beelzebub."

The door sighed open and a pale faced trio of passengers emerged on unsteady legs into a large brightly lit open plan office suite where half a dozen demons were – with a clatter of clawed nails on keypads – sat busily entering data into desk top computers.

"How may I be of assistance?" The honeyed words came from the rouge-red full lipped mouth of a stunning blond cream skinned woman with a cute little button nose, who was sat at a separate work station.

The woman rose to her feet and moved out from behind her desk.

Herbert's eyes opened a little wider in order to take in more fully her details.

She wore flame red 'very' skimpy hot pants and a skin tight white v-neck t-shirt that was coming under considerable strain as two enchanting mini mountains of flesh fought to escape their close confinement as she 'jiggled' over in their direction on her four inch heel, white leather thigh length boots.

The fact that she had tiny horns on her head and a small tail that ended in a little barb poking out the back of her hot pants...almost failed to register with Herbert.

Wanda nearly shot her one of those

looks that women usually reserved for pneumatic blond bimbos; instead she forced a weak smile.

"Good day," she said. "My colleagues and I are here on the authority of Lord Lucifer to look into problems relating to Hell's laundry."

"Lord Lucifer?"

"Indeed," Wanda said as she tapped the ID card on her chest. "As you can see, our passes include Lord Lucifer's personal sigil." The woman took a closer look then nodded.

"Very well, if you would just wait here a few moments, I will check if Lord Beelzebub can see you." Wanda nodded and repeated her weak, half hearted smile.

The 'bimbo' jiggled her way over to a closed door, rapped lightly and after waiting a few seconds, turned the door knob and entered. A full minute passed before she re-emerged and holding the door open signalled for them to enter.

Wanda and Henry filed quickly in, while Herbert took his time squeezing past the substantial partial obstruction.

Inside, the gargantuan figure rose from behind his desk and 'rumbled' at them. The rumbling became words that said: "You are here on Lord Lucifer's orders?" Wanda swallowed nervously.

"Yes Sir, my colleagues are renowned experts and they are here to check out if the laundry problem that is plaguing Hell perhaps has its origins in this Sector..."

"Why my Sector?"

"We have to check every Sector Sir." Beelzebub raised a huge paw of a hand and swatted away a mini swarm of flies that, some seven or eight feet from the floor, were circling around his ears.

"And what do you want from me?" he rumbled. Wanda shook her head.

"Nothing really Sir. It is just protocol that we should call on you first as soon as we arrived." Beelzebub nodded ponderously.

"Protocol. Good. You may go about your business now...my lunch is almost due," he said to an accompanying seismic rumbling from his enormous stomach. Wanda nodded.

"Thank you Sir, but before we go could I trouble you for your sigil on a pass allowing us unlimited access?" Beelzebub frowned.

"You have Lord Lucifer's sigil."

"Yes Sir, but You are Lord here and Your sigil surely must carry more weight than even Lord Lucifer's?"

"Very well," Beelzebub said as another seismic rumbling issued from his stomach.

"See my secretary on your way out."

"Oh my goodness!" Henry exclaimed

once they had gotten the pass and were stood outside the office. "He must be about eight feet tall and weigh about eighty stone!" Herbert nodded.

"Yeah well, his big sin was Gluttony after all..."

"And all those flies," Henry said. I wonder if they are like...a permanent accessory."

"Of course, he is Lord of the Flies."

"And what about that secretary. She had horns and a bloody tail!"

"Succubus," Herbert said patiently.

"Pardon?"

"A demon whose job it is to tempt men into sex."

"Oh right." Henry said.

"Blond Bimbo," Wanda said icily, Henry nodded, but thought *wow, I bet she's good at her job!* Wanda glanced at him and he decided to erase that thought from his mind and replace it with something oral and very innocently practical.

"So where do we go now?" He asked no one in particular. Herbert shrugged.

"Better ask our superior..." Wanda gave him a flinty look, as she was still a little peeved at only being made a Grade Two Liaison Officer.

"We need to get hold of Beelzebub's second in command and try to quiz him, anyone below that level will obviously be out of the loop."

"Makes sense," Henry muttered. "So lead on Madam McDuff." Wanda frowned and stroked a cheek in thought.

"One of us has to go back in and quiz the blond Bimbo," she said coolly.

"I'll do it!" Herbert said bravely.

"Thought you might," Wanda replied.

Back in the office Herbert made his way over to the Secretary's work station. "Sorry to bother you again pretty lady," he said, "But perhaps you could help us out with some information?" The succubus raised an eyebrow at the 'pretty lady' bit; then smiled seductively.

"Information?" she said silkily. "Are you sure that is all you require?" Herbert took a long breath and was glad that his halo was out of the picture.

"Well, another time I could think of any number of other things you might help me with beautiful lady...but unfortunately duty calls... by the way, what's your name...in case I need to get in contact with you urgently while we are down here?"

"Tanith," she purred, as the upgrade from 'pretty lady' to 'beautiful lady' registered.

"What information do you require," she added huskily.

Chapter 20

"Right," Herbert crowed. "Tanith has given me the name of Beelzebub's number two demon, Balan. So, if Beelzebub is involved in a plot this Balan, will surely be in on it too."

"Brilliant!" Henry said. "But how are we going to approach him. We can hardly go up to him and say 'excuse me but has Beelzebub mentioned anything to you about a plot to overthrow Lucifer.'" Wanda shook her head slowly in a 'You Silly Boy' fashion.

"Of course not. We need a bit of *Headology*. And if you two don't mind me saying, I think that a rapier approach that comes from a woman, rather than a blunderbuss approach from a mere man, is what is needed." Herbert sniffed.

"Thank Him," he said softly. "That you weren't made up to a Grade One Liaison Officer. You might then have got a little bit up yourself." Wanda favoured him with an obviously insincere big smile.

"Thank you for that observation Herbert. But let's concentrate on this Balan character." Herbert nodded.

"Balan, who apparently holds the title Grand Demon is the chief whip cracker and arse poker – with a pitchfork, I hasten to add – in Sector 1A."

"And how do we get to Sector 1A?"

"We have a scaled down Sector map secured, with a little bit of *Headology* and male flannel...from that 'blond bimbo'."

"Well done, Herbert, Wanda mouthed flatly."

"Thank you, Wanda," Herbert replied politely as he removed a folded up piece of paper from a breast pocket in his boiler suit and opened it out.

"Right, we have about a half mile of corridors to negotiate, plus two lifts, before we reach ground zero, where we take a shuttle to a city by the name of"...he squinted at his map... "Helot." Henry blinked.

"Ground Zero...Shuttle...A City named Helot...Are you saying we actually go Outside!"

"Of course we go outside. You don't think the whole of this Sector and its millions of inhabitants is housed in a giant bloody building do you?"

"I don't know... I sort of thought that the whole of Hell was just one big cave thing with fire and stuff..." Herbert shook his head.

"Henry; do you have any idea of the population of Hell?"

"Well no, of course not..."

"Well it's probably something similar

to the number of grains of sand on Bridlington Beach."

"Oh, right; so what about our first trip down to Hell; are you saying that had an 'outside' as well?"

"Of course. You don't think Old Nick and his senior demons spend all their time cooped up in those shit conditions do you! Hell no! They live in the suburbs where there are some very desirable properties I can tell you!"

"Well I never!"

"You don't say…"

***

"Ground Zero," Herbert said as they fetched up at a large smoked glass window that had a sign above it that said, in what Henry had begun to accept as Hell's standard type face: **Shuttle Service.**

Herbert pressed a button at the side of the window and it slide noiselessly open to reveal a covered concourse that was packed with miserable looking residents and a large number of demons, who were diligently prodding away with their pitchforks in an effort to create some sort of order.

One of the demons held a loud hailer to his mouth and in what passed as a polite request in Hell barked: "Right you fucking turds, get into your queues below your destination letter now...before I have your fucking bowels ripped out with rusty bayonets!" The request received an immediate response as a stampede began in the direction of the said destination letters.

"Come on," Herbert said. "Letter 'H' for Helot; and look lively or else you are likely to get a bleedin' great fork up your jacksie!"

They jostled their way through to the letter 'H' without encountering any pitchforks or rusty bayonets and joined a queue of about two dozen people standing next to a battered parked single-decker bus. The driver, an imp, was standing on his seat reading a copy of the *Hades Herald* he had spread out across the steering wheel. He was making a very successful attempt at totally ignoring his waiting passengers.

"What's he playing at!" Herbert moaned ten minutes later when their erstwhile driver had managed to turn only one page of the paper.

"Maybe he's word blind," Henry offered. The driver glanced across at the waiting queue, pushed his oversized peaked hat up a little until it sat just behind his horns, took a stubby pencil out of his jacket pocket, licked the lead and slowly turned the page over.

"Oh shit," Herbert moaned. "Word blind or not the little sod is only about to tackle the bloody crossword!"

An hour later the imp folded the paper, glanced out of the window at the queue; then proceeded to take out the makings for a roll up, which he ended up smoking extremely slowly. Herbert began jumping up and down on the spot.

The driver took the quarter inch dimp from his mouth, had a good look at it to see if he could manage at least one more drag, shook his head and swallowed it (the dimp not his head).

"About bloody time!" Herbert shouted up at the window. The imp glanced down at him...and took out the makings for a second roll up.

Ten minutes later and Herbert had built up a head of steam sufficient to hurl the *Flying Scotsman* from Euston to Edinburgh at two hundred mph.

"Don't say a word!" Henry ordered Herbert as the second dimp disappeared down the little imp's throat. Herbert bit his lip. The imp, with head tilted sideways and a quizzical look on his face, glanced down at Herbert. Herbert bit down harder; just before there was a whoosh of air and the bus door slid open.

The passengers began filing in,

showing their tickets as they made their way to the seats.

"Ticket," the driver said to Herbert, who had fair jumped up the bus steps.

"Ticket?" Herbert said slowly.

"Ticket," the imp repeated.

"We don't have tickets," Herbert said.

"Then fuck off," the imp replied.

"Now listen here you little fu..." Henry stepped up quickly.

"Excuse me driver," he said pleasantly. "We don't have tickets because we are here on behalf of Lord Lucifer and Lord Beelzebub." Henry pointed to his ID badge.

"Oh, right, the imp said after taking a close look at the badge. "Why didn't you say that an hour and a half ago and I would've opened the door."

They took their seats at the front of the bus and there was a 'ding' as a 'fasten seat' belt sign lit up.

Henry looked at Herbert, who shrugged. "I know," he said. "I'd be surprised if this old crate could do more than twenty miles an hour." Henry was about to reply when the driver pressed a button on the steering wheel, there was a sound like a Jumbo Jet engine firing up, a twenty foot long jet of flame shot out from the bus' rear end and his head and body slammed backwards into the seat as the vehicle catapulted forward.

"Ooohhh My G...!" He yelled as the not so well guided missile shot across the concrete surface towards a huge set of sliding doors...that were shut.

"Brake!" he screamed. The imp, from his position standing on the driver's seat turned around.

"Break what?" he said.

"The brakes; the fucking brakes!"

"What brakes?" The imp said as the sliding doors began to (slowly) slide apart. Henry squeezed his eyes shut as a flashback to an Austrian *piste* and a huge spruce tree seared itself into his brain. He waited for the crash...that didn't come.

He opened his eyes slowly. They were outside! And the bus was barrelling down an arrow straight black tarmac road under an angry orange/red sky.

He closed his eyes again and took a long and very deep breath as the trip hammer inside his chest began to slow down to something approaching normal pace.

"That was a bit hairy." Herbert said. Henry opened his eyes.

"A bit hairy, Herbert?' My G...Goodness man, it was bloody terrifying!"

"You're not used to this not dying again thing yet are you Henry?" Henry took another deep breath.

"It's not the dying that bothers me, because now I know I can't permanently die, it's the physical trauma and agony that comes with not dying again when the brain tells me I should be dying again!"

"Oh right; get you...I think."

Henry shook his head slowly then looked out of the window again. "It's a desert, with cactuses... cacti," he corrected himself.

"Yeah, pretty desolate alright. Wonder how far away this *Helot* place is?" Herbert mused. Wanda, who had been quiet a surprisingly long time for a woman, chipped in.

"Check the map. It's probably drawn to scale with one of those little bar things at the bottom that shows how many inches to the thingy." Herbert sniffed.

"I was just about to do that as it happens."

He took out and unfolded the map onto his lap. "Right, according to the scale it's about twenty miles; so at the speed this lunatic driver is doing we should be there in about two minutes."

Chapter 21

The city loomed into sight dead ahead.
"Looks pretty big," Henry said, taking in the
large cluster of tall tower blocks and the
proliferation of smaller buildings that
surrounded them.

A minute later and they were almost
on top of it. "He needs to start slowing
down," Herbert mused," as the 'fasten seat
belt' sign *pinged*. "Or we'll end up in
someone's front garden!"

Buckled up, Henry grasped his seat's
arm rests tightly as an immediate impact
became almost inevitable.

"Ohhh sugar!" he yelled as the imp -
with the vehicle literally yards from a
concrete wall - hauled on the steering wheel
and with a scream of tortured rubber the bus
slewed into a tight semi circle before lurching
sideways, turning over and rolling twice,
before coming to a stop upside down with its
wheels spinning madly and farting flame
from its exhaust pipe.

There was several seconds of total
silence before a chorus of shouts, groans,
moans and expletives filled the air. Then
there was a *ping*. Everyone stopped what they

were doing, in time to hear a pleasant recorded female voice declare "Please remain seated and with your seat belt securely fastened until the vehicle has come to a complete stop. If the vehicle has by chance already stopped and you are currently upside down, please remain so until the recovery crew arrive to right the vehicle.

"We trust you have had a pleasant journey and *Hell's Hot Wheels* look forward to travelling with you again..." *Ping*.

A dangling Henry craned his neck to look out of a now shattered window. "They are on their way," he said, as a line of brawny demons came trotting into view.

The 'recovery crew' lined up down one side of the bus and at an order from their foreman of "Bend" they bent forward in practiced unison. "Arms out hands under," the foreman sang. "Hands grip." Hands gripped. "HEAVE!" They heaved and with a groan followed by the sound of breaking window glass the bus flipped onto its side.

"Stand Easy," the foreman ordered. Then pointing to the demon nearest the bus door he said "That man, inside, seatbelts disengage!" The nominated demon wrenched the door open and vaulted inside. There then followed a series of clicks, followed by the thump of falling bodies and angry shouts of "get off me you twat!" as passengers suspended on the 'high side' fell onto passengers on the 'low side'.

"Bloody Hell," Henry said as they stood together at the roadside. "As a welcome to *Helot* that arrival takes some beating!" Herbert nodded.

"You're not wrong there squire; but tell you what, that recovery crew certainly knew what they were doing hey?"

"Probably had plenty of practice," Henry replied, looking sourly at the imp driver who was sat on a concrete bench casually smoking another roll up.

Together, the passengers walked, limped, hobbled; or in two cases, were carried on stretchers to the bus depot building. Inside, Wanda led Henry and Herbert to an Information Desk manned by a bored looking woman who was filing her finger nails.

"Excuse me." Wanda said.

"I have no idea," the woman replied without looking up.

"Pardon?"

"Whatever you are going to ask me, I have no idea."

"This is an Information Desk isn't it?"

"Yeah."

"And your job is to impart information isn't it?" The woman put her file down and examined her nails.

"Suppose so..." Wanda's face took on an angry red glow.

"Now you listen to me you piece of shit. You see this badge on my chest; it carries the personal sigil of Lord Lucifer! Now I suggest you stop looking at your fucking nails and start doing your job, before you find yourself on a gibbet getting hung drawn and quartered!"

The woman's eyes shot open and she stammered out an apology. Wanda smiled thinly.

"So do I take it," she said sweetly, "that you do impart information on request?"

"Yes Mam!"

"Good. Then please tell me where I can get in touch with Grand Demon Balan; if that is not too much trouble of course."

"No trouble at all Mam! The Grand Demon's office is in the Aleister Crowley Building on Elm Street."

"And Elm Street?"

"Out the main entrance, turn left and about two hundred metres on the right... Mam!"

"Thank you."

"You're very welcome Mam!"

Outside, Henry whistled in admiration.

"Wow Wanda, that was amazing!" Wanda shrugged.

"I spent time in the, er, company of

some strong willed men over the last few years before my death. Men, who never suffered fools; so maybe a bit of that has rubbed off somewhere...Anyway, turn left and about two hundred metres on the right she said, so let's go."

"Jah Mon Capitan," Herbert said, adding a smart salute.

***

The Aleister Crowley Building was an imposingly huge stainless steel and black tinted glass pyramid shaped edifice that dominated Elm Street.

"Looks like a perfect place to find a Grand Demon," Henry mused as they mounted the half dozen wide black marble steps that led to a large and slowly revolving glass door.

Inside, they made their way over to a reception desk where Wanda muttered almost under her breath: "Blond Bimbo Ahead."

The Receptionist was blond. She was also the double of the last 'blond bimbo' that Wanda had laid eyes on; except her hot pants were cerise instead of red and her white t-shirt was scoop neck rather than v-neck. That said, she was also wearing four inch heel, thigh length white leather boots.

Herbert made to step forward but Wanda held out an arm.

"Down boy," she said firmly. "I'll handle this one."

The receptionist smiled lightly as Wanda approached then opened her mouth, but before she could speak Wanda beat her to it.

"My colleagues and I are here to speak with Grand Demon Balan. Tell him that emissaries from Lords Lucifer and Beelzebub are waiting to see him."

"Please hold on a moment while I see if Grand Demon Balan is available..." She dialled a number and after a few seconds Wanda heard someone on the other end pick up.

"Reception Sir," the receptionist said. "There are emissaries from Lords Lucifer and Beelzebub who wish to speak with you."

"Yes Sir, I will send them up right away." She put the telephone down, reached into a desk drawer and took out a slim black plastic oblong and passed it to Wanda.

"This will get you into the private lift on the right. Press for the top floor and Grand Demon Balan's office is directly opposite the lift door." Wanda nodded and turned to Henry and Herbert. "Right gentlemen," she said coolly, "The Grand Demon awaits."

Chapter 22

"First thing he will want to know is why Lucifer has sent us," Wanda said as the lift began to rise. "So I will hesitate for a second or two to see if he looks a little nervous. If he does that might indicate that he has something to hide; such as being party to a plot."

"Or," Herbert said, "It might just mean that he is shit scared of the Big Man." Wanda shrugged.

"Maybe, but in any case it is worth it, just in case he does have something to hide."

"And what then?" Herbert asked.

"Then I will tell him about the laundry problem and that Lord Beelzebub has also backed our visit with a signed pass. Then if he and Lord Beelzebub are part of the plot that will put him at ease by thinking we are only interested in laundry."

"So keep him guessing hey," Henry said admiringly.

"Well, it should keep us one step ahead."

Any more conversation was then stopped by an announcement from the lift that said they had arrived at the top floor and at the Grand Demon's Office.

They took collective deep breaths as the lift door slid open.

"Right," Wanda whispered, as she reached out to an intercom panel mounted at the side of the door. "We are here on legitimate business, so cool heads are the order of the day." She pressed a button and a buzzing sound announced that an electronic unlocking mechanism had been activated. She pushed the door open and they filed through into a reception area manned by another of the 'bimbo' clones. Wanda sighed.

"I believe the Grand Demon is expecting us," she said in a no nonsense officious tone of voice. The succubus rose from her seat and she, not surprisingly, was wearing hot pants, a skimpy t-shirt and four inch heel, thigh length white leather boots. Her hot pants were shocking pink as was her t-shirt. *I wonder how many of these bimbos there are*, Wanda thought. *'Cause apart from the standard white leather thigh length boots - which must be de rigueur down here - they must soon run out of sexy colour combinations.*

"Please walk this way," the receptionist said as she sashayed over to a door. Herbert copied her walk, but a killer look from Wanda put a quick stop to his antics.

The cloned 'bimbo' rapped on the

door, opened it and ushered them through. Herbert squeezed past very slowly.

The seated Grand Demon, who bore a passing resemblance to a week old corpse didn't bother standing up. Instead, he fixed the newcomers with a cold fish eyed stare.

"You are here on behalf of Lord Lucifer?" Balan said evenly. Wanda nodded.

"Yes Sir my colleagues and I have been given leave by Lord Lucifer to visit the Sectors and Lord Beelzebub has also ratified Lord Lucifer's decision." She studied the Grand Demon's face closely as she spoke.

"And what is the reason for your visit to the Sectors?"

Wanda hesitated for a handful of seconds.

"Well Sir, you may have noticed that there is an ingrained problem regarding the efficacy of the laundry system down here..."

"You are here because our laundry is not sparking white and bright!" Wanda nodded and looked for any sign of relief on the Grand Demon's face. She saw only puzzlement.

"Yes Sir," she said seriously. "Lord Lucifer in particular sees the problem as a serious one." Balan nodded slowly.

"Well then," he said. "If Lord Lucifer sees the problem as serious, then who am I to take a different view?"

"Indeed Sir. And hopefully my colleagues, who are specialists, will be able to ascertain whether the source of the problem is centred on this particular Sector." The Grand Demon shrugged.

"Very well, so what do you need from me to help you in your endeavours?"

"Only your written permission to allow us free passage anywhere in your Sector Sir."

"You already carry the ultimate permission; that given by Lord Lucifer and backed up by Lord Beelzebub."

"True Sir, but 1A is your domain and your word obviously carries more weight than any other here." Balan nodded slowly.

"And Lord Lucifer; you were given leave by him personally to undertake this venture?"

"Yes Sir." The Grand Demon ran his tongue briefly over his lips.

"And Lord Lucifer, did he perhaps mention my name in your discussions?"

"He did indeed Sir. He said that you were Lord Beelzebub's most trusted associate and that you were a demon highly regarded over at Hell's Head Office."

Wanda studied Balan's reaction to her words closely and was pleased to notice a definite look of self pride flit briefly across his face.

"Lord Lucifer said that did he?"

"He did Sir."

"Well, it is nice to be appreciated. Perhaps when you return to Head Office you might pass on my best wishes to him?" Wanda nodded.

"You may be assured of that Sir."

"Good," the Grand Demon said smoothly as he opened a drawer in his desk, took out a sheet of parchment paper, picked up a pen and wrote out a brief letter of permission, to which he added his signature. He handed it to Wanda and said "You will remember to pass on my regards to Lord Lucifer?"

"Of course Sir; and thank you for your very kind assistance."

The Grand Demon waved Wanda's thanks away, pressed a buzzer on his desk and the blond bimbo sashayed back into the room to escort them out.

In the lift Wanda turned to Henry and Herbert. "He has no knowledge of any plot," she said firmly.

"How can you tell that from a brief conversation?" Henry asked. She nodded.

"I studied his face and when I mentioned that Lucifer held him in high regard he nearly hopped around like the toady he is.

"Believe me, he knows nothing of any plot and so, with him being Beelzebub's trusted number two, we can be pretty sure that Beelzebub's not a prime mover either."

"Don't you think that might be a leap of faith too far?" Henry said.

"Trust me Henry, I'm a woman, and if women are good at anything, it's spotting when a man is trying to hide something."

"Okay," Herbert said slowly. "But just to make things look kosher it's probably best if we spend a bit of time checking on pipes and ball cocks and things before making our way back to Sector 1 Head Office and the Super Express Lift." Henry bridled.

"What, you mean we jump aboard another one of those *Hell's Hot Wheels* non-death, death traps!" Wanda hesitated a second.

"No, we flash our badges and written authorisation and commandeer a taxi."

Chapter 23

Wanda eyed up the destination buttons on the SEL panel. "Lord Beelzebub, Sector 1 was Floor 100," she said. "And Lord Leviathan, Sector 2, is Floor 200." She raised a hand and prodded a button. Henry closed his eyes.

"That wasn't so bad was it?" Wanda said a minute later to a pale faced Henry; who replied with a groan followed by a successful attempt at re-swallowing his last meal.

The lift door slid open and they stepped out into a large nautical themed room. The walls were lined with wicked looking harpoons, stuffed swordfish and killer whale heads and giant paintings of various monsters rising from the deep; while in a non gruesome vain, the ceiling was festooned with fishing nets fitted with variously coloured glass ball floats.

"So, he sometimes assumes the shape of a great sea monster, I take it," Henry said.

"He does indeed," Herbert replied adding, "In fact he apparently gets a big kick out of attacking and sinking any fishing boats he comes across... along with all hands on board." Henry frowned.

"If he drowns everyone, how do they, get the bodies back to, like un-drown them then?"

"I've heard that he has a crack squad of Demon aqua divers who do that and any they can't find just eventually float to the surface anyway." Henry shuddered.

"And I bet those ones are a pretty sight after spending ages being nibbled at by all manner of sea creatures!"

"Yeah, suppose so. Anyway come on let's check out that door over there," Herbert said nodding towards the opposite end of the room.

The door was unlocked and they opened it to find themselves on the threshold of another large room. This one had one particularly striking feature. The whole of one wall was taken up by a huge glass window that looked out onto a picturesque harbour full of what was obviously a fleet of fishing boats... Oh, and it also had a blond bimbo clone who was sitting behind a workstation. *Apple green hot pants, red t-shirt and, of course, four inch heel, thigh length white leather boots*, Wanda thought, before adding a sigh.

As she strode over to deliver her usual introduction the woman looked up from her computer and smiled thinly. "How may I..."

she managed before Wanda, irked by yet another blond bimbo, launched into her delivery, which ended with her flashing her ID badge.

"Lord Leviathan is presently at sea and is not expected back for some time," the bimbo said.

"Very well, but while we are waiting perhaps you would direct us to his second in command."

"Grand Demon Valafar has an office on the second floor."

"Good, then call him and announce our arrival." Henry shook his head slowly while thinking *Blimey she has got the flinty faced harridan look off to a bloody tee!*

The bimbo made the call, making sure she relayed the visitors' highly official standing, then said

"Grand Demon Valafar will see you now madam. You and the gentlemen can take the lift to the second floor in the corridor through there," she indicated a door. "And the Grand Demon's door is the one that has a skull that serves as a knocker nailed to it."

"A bloody skull nailed to the door!" Henry said as they stood next to the lift.

"Maybe it's just a plastic one," Herbert said none too convincingly.

It certainly did not look plastic and Henry flinched slightly as he lifted the jawbone and delivered a gentle rat-a-tat-tat, while half expecting to hear the rattle of falling teeth hitting the floor.

"Enter!" a funereal bass voice demanded.

Wanda moved an easily shifted Henry aside and led the way in.

Grand Demon Valafar was obviously a very tall individual, as sitting at his desk he still towered head and shoulders over Henry, who immediately mentally christened him 'Frankie'...after a monster that had sometimes rampaged through his dreams as a child.

His huge head had a decidedly square look about it and this was reinforced by black hair that was cut into a ragged fringe that ended some three inches above a wide and broad expanse of forehead.

All that was missing as far as Henry could see was a nine inch bolt through his neck.

"You are emissaries of Lord Lucifer?" Valafar intoned in what could be described as a funereal tone of voice.

"Yes Sir and thank you for seeing us at such short notice," Wanda replied. The Grand Demon waved a huge hand in dismissal; and for an instant Henry was almost sure that he saw a dotted line of suture marks around the giant's wrist.

"Emissaries of the Supreme Lord are entitled to immediate access no matter when, and without notice."

"A very commendable attitude Sir. And are you well acquainted with Lord Lucifer?" Wanda said brightly. The Grand Demon shook his monstrous head.

"I have never had the honour of meeting the Supreme Lord. My station is perhaps too humble..." Wanda tutted.

"Surely not Sir! Lord Lucifer himself mentioned your name before we set out from Head Office." Valafar's eyes opened wide.

"The Supreme Lord spoke my name!"

"He did indeed Sir."

"And He said what?" Wanda hesitated for a second.

"He said that if we got to meet you we had to pass on his good wishes for the sterling work you are doing in this Sector."

The Grand Demon's face, one that only a blind mother could love, broke into a frankly, unsettling, grin.

"I am most gratified," he said humbly.

The desk phone rang as Valafar stopped speaking. He picked it up and listened for a few seconds before putting it back on its cradle.

"Lord Leviathan is returning. So if there is anything more you require of me please ask." Wanda shook her head.

"No Sir, we have passed on Lord Lucifer's regards and our conversation has been most enlightening."

Back in the lift Henry shook his head. "Grand Demon?" He said. "More like something from The Walking Dead!"

"Yes," Wanda agreed, "But I didn't spot any sign of a hidden agenda, did you?"

"No, but having said that, I don't think I have your nose for it..."

They made their way through the trophy and fishing net room, opened the door to the reception room...and stopped dead.

The panoramic window which on their earlier visit had been displaying a typical harbour scene with boats gently bobbing at anchor had been transformed to a scene from HELL.

"Oh my G...!" Henry gasped as his eyes fastened onto the scene playing out in the harbour. He saw a monstrous giant squid like creature towering above the fishing boats. Tiny figures were leaping from decks into the suddenly churned up waves and through the window he could just make out the sound of terrified screams.

The monster snaked out a tentacle, ripped a boat from its mooring and hurled it half a mile at least out to sea, where it sank immediately without trace.

Back in the harbour it let out a roar

which rattled the window before smashing a mighty oak tree thick tentacle onto the deck of another boat, shearing it clean in half.

"Looks like Lord Leviathan is in a bit of a mood," the bimbo said glancing out the window at the carnage, before returning to her computer.

Henry, Wanda and Herbert exchanged stunned looks.

"A bit of a mood?" Henry whispered, before expelling a long slow breath. The bimbo looked up from her computer.

"He'll be fine in a minute," she said matter-of-factly. "Just likes to let them know who the head honcho is now and again."

No sooner had she spoken, when the monster, apparently sated, subsided and sank lower into the water before, with a slow and sinuous swirl of its tentacles it began to swim towards the shore.

As the water became shallower more and more of its scaly grey brown body emerged, and the watchers witnessed a remarkable metamorphosis.

The huge cruel beaked head shrank and slowly took on human proportions. Two of the thick rubbery tentacles shrank to become well muscled human arms and the thick shapeless body became a much smaller, but well sculpted chest and six pack loaded abdomen.

Shallower still and two more tentacles were transformed into legs and the creature waded rather than swam.

It reached the shore, strode onto land and shook itself. And as the water cascaded off its shoulder length black curly hair Wanda could not help but notice that a fifth and shorter tentacle was dangling between its tree trunk legs. She looked much closer and realised that what she thought was a tentacle was certainly not a tentacle!

"Oh my!" she muttered under her breath as the 'all man' began to walk towards the window.

The bimbo rose from her desk and excused herself with the words, "I'll just let Lord Leviathan in, won't be a tick."

Wanda raised her hands to her hips and slowly smoothed out the creases in her mini skirt.

Within a minute the bimbo returned followed by a six foot six inch, Adonis who was briskly towelling his naked body. Wanda checked on the tentacle again, just to make sure that it wasn't...a tentacle. It wasn't.

"Tanith tells me you are emissaries of Lord Lucifer," the Adonis said. Wanda nodded, but even while her attention was elsewhere a little voice inside her head chipped in with *Tanith? All the bimbos must have the same bloody name!* She dismissed the distracting little voice.

"Yes Sir, we are," she said making sure that her eyes were focussed on his and not anywhere else. *Hell*, the obstinate little voice in her head said, *He has gorgeous green eyes!* She swallowed, smiled lightly and forced herself to mentally answer the voice with *It's not his real body; he's probably a hoary wrinkled two thousand year old wreck with no teeth and a case of galloping halitosis.*

The Adonis finished his brisk towelling. "So," he said, brightly, "How is old Lucifer. Still giving every one Hell over at Head Office?"

"As far as I know, yes Sir and I guess that's what his job description calls for." Leviathan smiled and nodded.

"Well put; and I should really get up there to see him again."

"Again Sir?

"Yes; must be ten years or so since we last met up for a chin wag."

"Really; that long Sir?" he nodded.

"At least that long. I think it was to celebrate his two thousandth birthday; or some such milestone."

"And the other Lords, do you meet up with them regularly?"

"Hell no! Can't do with all the preening and posing from that bunch of tossers! Anyway forget them; what does my old mate Lucifer want?"

"Well Sir, you may not know it but all Hell is having problems with its laundry and Lucifer has recruited us," she indicated Henry and Herbert, "to see if we can find the source of the problem." Leviathan shrugged.

"A laundry problem," he said, adding another shrug. "Doesn't make much difference to me. Spend most of my time in the sea anyway; so not really used to wearing clothes, laundered and ironed or not." Wanda allowed herself to lower her gaze for a second or two.

"No Sir. And may I say that *au natural* suits you very well." He smiled.

"Thanks, and anything you need, just give me a shout." Wanda shook her head slowly.

"Thank you Sir, but I think we will just take some time checking on the plumbing and such in this Sector, before reporting back to Lord Lucifer."

Leviathan nodded and flashed a mouthful of perfect blindingly white teeth.

"Very well," he said pleasantly. "Now if you will excuse me I have some paperwork to attend to in my office." Wanda smiled back and as Lord Leviathan turned to leave them, she casually took in his cute, tight little bum, before turning her attention briefly to the blond bimbo.

"We are going now," she said coolly. "But before we do I want to leave you with a little friendly advice." Blondie cocked her head to one side.

"Yes?" She said. Wanda glanced down at the bimbo's t-shirt and skimpy hot pants.

"The advice is simple. When it comes to dress, Red and Green should never be seen."

Later in the Super Express Lift, Wanda casually said: "Lord Leviathan seemed to be quite pleasant... for a Demon, didn't he?"

"Quite pleasant? Yes I suppose so... for a homicidal maniac who enjoys smashing ships to bits and drowning people," Henry said flatly.

He had noticed Wanda's lingering glances at the Demon's nether regions.

Chapter 24

Wanda reached up. "Next stop, Lord Mammon; also known as *The Lord of Avarice*," she said, then, after checking that Henry was strapped in, she reached up to prod the relevant button.

"You must be getting used to plunging down lift shafts," Wanda said a minute later as she checked Henry's non-white face when the lift door opened. He smiled thinly and was about to answer, when Herbert said. "Wow, get a load of this place!"

The lift had deposited them in a reception room that dripped with OTT chic.

They strode out onto black marble floor tiles that were shot with gold flecks. The black walls were lined with crimson velvet drapes. There was a life sized bronze, spot lit statue of a horned demon, in the process of sticking it to a cowering man...and there was the usual blond bimbo sat behind a work station.

Wanda let out an exasperated sigh; *Looks like Gods, Devils and Men think alike when it comes to their idea of a sexy woman,* she thought. *But it is what it is,* she mused adding a mental shrug. *And at least this one does show*

an ounce of class with her silk gold lame' t-shirt
and hot pants; even if the effect is almost ruined
by those bloody tarty white leather thigh length
boots...

"Yes, you can help us," Wanda said quickly before the bimbo could do more than open her redder than red pouting lips.

She reeled off her well rehearsed introduction, finishing off with a firm request for an immediate audience with Lord Mammon. The bimbo blinked and reached for the telephone at her elbow.

"You were sent by Lord Lucifer?" the tall thin sallow faced man said in a voice that for some reason reminded Wanda of the rustling together of several sheets of very dry paper .

"Yes Sir, by Lord Lucifer and helped on our way with the good wishes of Lord Beelzebub and Lord Leviathan."

"And what is Lord Lucifer's reason for sending you to this Sector?" Wanda shook her head.

"Not to just this Sector sir, we are charged with visiting every Sector."

"And again; I ask for the reason." Wanda delayed her answer for a few seconds in order to study Mammon's face.

"The reason is to look closely into a problem that is perplexing Lord Lucifer; one that he is very keen to resolve..." She paused again for a few seconds, before seeing a look of exasperation spreading across his hatchet thin face. She continued quickly.

"There is a problem that has spread to every Sector. It involves Hell's Laundries." Mammon, frowned.

"Hell's Laundries?"

"Yes Sir, I am sure that you have noticed how the laundry service is failing to live up to set standards..."

"Set standards?" Mammon shook his head slowly.

"Yes Sir, to put it bluntly Hell's whites are turning out anything but ..."

"Anything but what?"

"Anything but...white." Mammon shook his head again and lifted a thin blue veined hand – that Wanda noted had a jewelled ring on all four of its fingers – and pointed to his chest.

"You will see young woman that I dress only in black, ergo I have no interest in white, or any shade thereof."

"Granted Sir, but I am sure you must agree that if Lord Lucifer has taken the problem to heart' then it behoves us all to do our best to help resolve it..." Mammon nodded slowly.

"Yes, you are right young woman. Lord Lucifer's will is paramount; so what do you need to do in my Sector?" Wanda hesitated again for a few seconds.

"You are obviously very busy yourself Sir, but it would help my colleagues and I if you would allow us to approach your second in command with a view to him showing us around the Sector's potential weak points that could allow any extraneous matter to infiltrate the water system."

"Very well; I will give you written permission to approach Count Raum, who will be at your disposal during your stay."

"Thank you Sir, and where will we find the Count?"

"Reception will give you directions."

They made their way back to the blond bimbo who quickly printed out directions to Count Raum's office, which was only five levels down, so they would only have to use a 'standard' lift and not – thankfully as far as Henry was concerned – the Super Express Lift. On their way Henry said "Well, what did you make of him?" Wanda shook her head.

"It didn't look to me like he was hiding anything; how about you two?" They both agreed with her, before Herbert said,

"Extraneous matter...Infiltrate the water system...Well done by the way!" Wanda nodded.

"Bullshit pinched from a master bull shitter..."

***

Count Raum also wore black. He didn't have any rings on his fingers; but what he did have was a rather dashing red silk lined cape and a pronounced east European accent.

"Welcome," he said steepling his fingers from behind the desk as they were ushered into his office by the ubiquitous bimbo; who, due to familiarity with the breed, Wanda hadn't even bothered to waste a sigh on.

"Lord Mammon has just spoken to me on the telephone of your mission," he said smoothly, before directing them to sit. "And vee are keen to assist," he added with a smile.

"Thank you Sir," Wanda replied as she took in his slicked back and black accentuated widow's peak... and the fact that his smile had exposed two rather large incisors in his upper jaw.

"So..."he raised a hand and languidly pointed a long nailed forefinger in Wanda direction.

"Er, Wanda Sir."

"Vonda, a lovely name for a lovely vuman."

"Er, Thank you sir," she replied, then swallowed nervously as she realised that he hadn't been making eye contact when he spoke. Rather he had been studying her neck.

"So, Vonda," he repeated, "You and your companions are laundry experts?" Wanda shook her head.

"I am not Sir, I am a mere Grade *Two* Liaison Officer. It is my colleagues who are experts."

Count Raum turned briefly towards Henry and Herbert and favoured them with a mere vertical tic of his head. Henry returned the gesture.

"And tell me Sir," Henry said, "Have you noticed a deterioration of the laundry service in this Sector?" The Count pursed his lips and shrugged.

"Laundry is of no concern to me. I haff much more important matters to think of."

"I am sure you do Sir. But you are aware aren't you that Lord Lucifer considers the laundry problem to be important?"

"Lord Mammon mentioned this yes."

"As a matter of interest Sir, how do you get on with Lord Lucifer?" Count Raum frowned lightly.

"Get on? Vot is 'get on'?"

"Your relationship with Lord Lucifer is it cordial?" Raum shook his head.

"I haff no relationship with Lord Lucifer. I meet him once at Centennial Meeting of Hell's Sectors, fifty years ago only I think."

"Oh, right. And Lord Mammon, I

suppose he meets Lord Lucifer on a more regular basis?"

"Ja, they haff been good friends for many century."

"Good friends eh?"

"Ja, they sometime eefen go on long weekend break together up in Heffen!"

"Well that is very interesting," Henry said. "And it is nice to see that Heaven and Hell can treat each other civilly, isn't it?"

"Ja, Eternity iss very long time to be pissed off with everybody..."

"Couldn't have put it better myself Sir!" Henry said. Wanda nodded agreement.

"Yes Sir;" she said firmly, " and as we are sure you have a very busy schedule, perhaps you can provide us with authorisation that will allow us to check out the tangential supply lines and header tanks in this Sector for any fractures?"

"You do not need personal attention more?"

"No Sir, I am sure we can manage somehow on our own."

"Vell, if you are sure," Count Raum said a little reluctantly, as he tilted his head slightly and fixed his eyes on Wanda's slender white neck.

Chapter 25

"Well, I reckon we have drawn another blank there," Henry muttered as they stood outside the door to the internal lift that would take them back up five floors to the Super Express Lift. Wanda sighed.

"Yes, I think you are right...and I'm beginning to think this is something of a wild demon chase."

"Cheer up," Herbert said brightly. "We've got Belphagor, Amon and Asmodeus to go...and my money is on Amon. He's a moody little shit by all accounts. And I bet he's just the type to get mixed up in a coup."

Back up five floors, Wanda wiped the coded key across the small red dimly backlit square of plastic next to the lift and the Super Express Lift door slid noiselessly open.

"Right," she said, "Next stop Lord Belphagor, who, if I recall Nosy Parker's description is one big lazy bastard and not a potential contestant for Mastermind."

"That's right, Hernry said. "But don't forget what else Nosy mentioned. He said we were to underestimate him and his fellow dimwit, Amon, at our peril, as what they might lack in grey matter they more than make up for in low cunning and single minded determination."

"Message received and committed to memory," Wanda said, adding: "Are you properly strapped in Henry?" Before she reached out to prod the relevant button.

***

Lord Belphagor's 'Slothful' nature was amply illustrated by the reception room that greeted them as the lift doors opened.

The floor was 'carpeted' in linoleum that had seen better centuries. The walls were clad with red flock (a la' 1970's Asian curry house) wallpaper; and the standard issue bimbo had obviously excelled herself in an effort to match the decor.

Her foundation and blusher looked like it had been applied with a trowel; her lipstick with a three inch horse hair paint brush. Her blond (black roots showing) hair looked as though a rat might at any second leap out of it and her black leather t-shirt and hot pants were well scuffed.

Perhaps the only saving grace about her appearance was her four inch heel tarty white leather thigh length boots; which actually looked rather smart when placed against the rest of the ghastly package.

"Yeah?" the bimbo said out of the

corner of a mouth that had a half smoked fag dangling from it. Wanda's own mouth hardened.

"Yeah?" she said "What fucking Charm School did you graduate from!"

"What?" Wanda took a deep breath.

"Let's start again shall we. You say: "Yes madam, can I help you?"

"What?"

"Oh for fuck's sake! Read this badge...You can read can't you?"

"Course I can read..."

"Good, well you will see that it bears the name and sigil of Lord Lucifer Himself."

"Oh, right."

"Oh, right. That means that we are not here to empty your waste basket - which incidentally is overflowing - We are here to see Lord Belphagor...immediately, concerning an urgent matter on the direct instruction of Lord Lucifer!"

"Oh, right," the bimbo said as she swept a pile of papers that were covering up her telephone onto the lino.

***

Lord Belphagor stifled a yawn as he waved them towards chairs and indicated they should sit. Wanda inclined her head and smiled lightly.

"Thank you Sir. You are obviously a very busy man, so we will not take up too much of your valuable time." He nodded.

"Yes, it can get most hectic in this Sector, what with problem solving and executive decision making. All that can be quite physically and mentally draining you know..."

"I'm sure it can be Sir. And you can also be sure that Lord Lucifer really appreciates your efforts."

"Lord Lucifer really appreciates my efforts you say?"

"Indeed he does Sir. Why he even went so far as to say that he wished some of the other Princes were as diligent as your good self... but please don't mention that to any of the other Princes Sir; we wouldn't want any jealous feelings to develop would we?"

"No, of course not. That would never do would it." Belphagor said as his chest swelled and his already expansive stomach threatened to send shirt buttons pinging across the room.

Wanda moved slightly to one side out of the line of fire before she said,

"As a matter of interest Sir, do you and Lord Lucifer go back a long way?" Belphagor's fleshy jowl wobbled as he nodded vigorously.

"A long way, maybe more than two thousand years."

"That long! My you must know him very well then."

"Always been good mates, me and him."

"Well then, I bet you are really annoyed by the rumours coming out of Head Office..." Belphagor frowned.

"What rumours?" Wanda raised a hand palm first.

"Oh, really Sir, please forget what I just said, some people just like to gossip..." Belphagor sent his jowl into wobbly jelly mode with another serious head shake.

"What rumours?" he repeated. Wanda sighed.

"Oh very well Sir, but as I said, people just like to gossip... So, rumour has it that Lord Lucifer and God are buddying up with each other these days..." Belphagor snorted.

"Bollocks!" he said forcefully. "They've been at each other's throats for thousands of years!"

"It's said they now have regular golf dates up in Heaven..."

"Bollocks! And even if they do, Lord Lucifer will have a good reason for it!"

"I am sure you are right Sir. Anyway, the reason that we are here at Lord Lucifer's request is to see if we can get to the bottom of the laundry problem..."

"Laundry problem...what laundry problem?"

"Ah, well Sir, perhaps you have been too busy to notice that all of the Sectors have been experiencing problems with the quality of their laundry services."

"Yes I must have been," Belphagor said slowly.

"Not to worry Sir. I don't think we need to trouble you more. Perhaps you could direct us to your second in command, who may not be as busy as your good self and is able to show us around the Sector."

"It is a big Sector," Belphagor mused. "So, perhaps you are right, seeing as how I am so busy."

He picked up a telephone and dialled a number. When the connection was made he said "Gressil, it's me, your boss. Listen, I am sending a little delegation from Lord Lucifer over to you.

"What? No it's not an annual audit. They just want you to show them around the Sector.

"Why? Oh some problem with the laundry or something."

He replaced the handset. "Right he will be pleased to show you around."

"And where will we find him Sir?" Wanda asked.

"See Tanith at reception, she'll direct you."

'*Tanith*', Wanda thought, with a weary mental sigh.

The helpful receptionist, Tanith, pulled out all the stops and managed to print out directions to Belphagor's Number Two, Gressil, and within a minute they were standing outside another internal lift.

"Ten levels down," Wanda said.

"But my gut feeling is that it will be a waste of time. I don't see Belphagor being our man. I think he is just too bone idle to get all het up about a coup." Henry and Herbert nodded.

"Probably right," Henry said. "So what do you think?" Wanda nodded.

"My vote is for making our way back to the SEL. and then on to your 'moody little shit', Amon, Herbert." Henry looked to Herbert, Herbert looked to Wanda and said:

"Moody little shit it is then."

Chapter 26

Amon's Sector was over 150 floors down from Belphagor's and after a good ninety second gravity defying plummet followed by a one second 'stop', the lift doors opened.

"That was a good one! Can we go back up and try it again?" Henry said as they exited. Wanda and Herbert looked sourly at him.

"You are joking aren't you?" Wanda said through clenched teeth.

"Yes, but I am getting used to it now. And I would never have thought I would say that!

"I once went on the Big Dipper at Blackpool and threw up on the very first dip right over this woman's head who was sitting in the car in front!"

"And now you're Hell's number One thrill seeker, amazing!"

"Yes, I think it was the Austrian ski slope that did it...that and the bloody great tree that did for me...must have scrambled some neurons or something..."

"Very illuminating," Herbert said as he stood outside a door that had a name plaque on it that read **Lord Amon,**
General of 60 Legions

"Sixty Legions?" What's that then? Henry said.

"A bloody lot of Demons," Herbert replied.

"But how many is sixty legions?" Henry said.

"Enough to start a bloody coup," I would think..." Herbert replied as he opened the door.

They entered a reception room that, while certainly more salubrious than Lord Belphagor's dump, was, never the less equally non typical of the general type.

It did not have bright or even slightly subdued lighting. It had downright dim lighting. The walls - which were tastefully decorated with mounted examples of weapons designed for slashing, decapitating, skewering, disembowelling and generally dealing out extreme discomfort - were uniformly black, as was the ceiling.

The only furniture in the room consisted of a large black workstation behind which was a single black chair...occupied by a Tanith.

This Tanith could have passed muster as a Warrior Queen. Her long blond hair was kept firmly in place by a wide black leather headband that was encrusted with half a dozen huge rubies. Her upper body was clad in a mid thigh length figure hugging t-shirt made out of light stainless steel chain mail that was cinched in at the waist by a broad black leather belt with a large silver buckle; and her muscular thighs, calf's and feet were clad in not white, but shiny black leather, four inch heel boots. Wanda was pleasantly surprised. *Maybe this bimbo is not a bimbo* she thought as she approached the workstation.

"Good day," she said civilly. The Amazon rose to her feet and looked down from her height at Wanda.

"Yes," she said slowly and deliberately, "it is a good day." Wanda, surprised at the response blinked.

"Yes, well, my colleagues and I are here at the request of Lord Lucifer himself."

"And?" the definitely non bimbo said coolly.

"And we need to speak with Lord Amon on an urgent matter."

"Lord Amon is engaged in battle planning."

"Pardon?"

"On the parade ground; he is overseeing manoeuvres..."

"And how long will these manoeuvres take?" The Amazon shrugged her broad shoulders.

"He has been engaged for three hours. Sometimes the manoeuvres last for a full day."

"Is he perhaps expecting a war?" Wanda said with the slightest hint of an edge to her tone. The Amazon shrugged again.

"Lord Amon is always prepared for any eventuality that might arise."

Bloody Hell, this one is one of a kind Wanda thought.

Herbert, who hadn't taken his eyes off the Amazon since they had entered, thought, *God, look at those nut cracker thighs!*

Henry, who was looking out of a large window as Wanda and the woman talked, thought *I wonder how many Legions those are down there... one, or the whole sixty...*

He coughed and cleared his throat. Wanda looked across at him and he pointed out the window. She looked.

"Good He...Hell!" she said as the spectacle of an enormous parade ground full almost to overflowing with thousands of naked red skinned, horned, huge pitchfork wielding demons assaulted her eyes.

As she watched, the shapeless multitude formed itself into dozens of equal sized blocks of perhaps five hundred individuals that then stood to attention as if waiting on a command. It was then that she first noticed a single non demon.

He wore golden armour in the style of a Roman General and was standing on a low dais looking out at the host. His right arm was raised on high and in his hand he held a sword that glinted crimson in the rays of the red sun. The man suddenly dropped his arm and the static scene burst into one of frantic clashing action, as block attacked block and then was attacked by another block.

Through the window Wanda could hear shouts of jubilation, screams of agony, as tridents found their mark.

The mad melee raged on for a full three minutes until suddenly, the golden figure raised its arm again and the scene froze. And as it did, hundreds of bodies were dragged clear and dumped at the side of the parade ground.

The blocks of demons re-grouped. The golden figure raised its arm again for a good minute...and then with a sudden downward swing, the action restarted.

"How often does he do that?" A shocked Wanda said as she locked her eyes onto the solitary 'human' figure.

"Twice a week, every week." Wanda nodded and turning from the scene of carnage, she swallowed and said:

"And can you get someone to tell him that a delegation from Lord Lucifer awaits him?"

"I could; but I won't."

"Why not?"

"Lord Amon is not one who takes

lightly to interruptions to his schedule..."

"What, not even for emissaries of Lord Lucifer!"

"Not even for emissaries of Lord Lucifer." Wanda took a deep breath. *This Amazon is not for turning* she thought.

"Very well, is there perhaps somewhere that we can wait in comfort for Lord Amon to return from his manoeuvres?"

"Yes, there is a visitor's suite. I will escort you there and send for you when Lord Amon can see you."

The suite reflected the reception room in decor, but without the wall art; nor of course, the resident Tanith.

"Bit sombre," Herbert said. "But comfortable enough," he added as he bounced lightly on a large black leather sofa.

Wanda, who was exploring the kitchen, raised her voice to let them know that she had found coffee and a percolator.

"Is it instant?" Henry shouted through.

"No, there are beans and a grinder."

"Good," Henry replied. "I can't stand that instant rubbish." As he said it he then thought: *'Listen to yourself Henry. You are dead; you are in Hell; you are on a secret spying mission that could have Heaven and Hell wide repercussions; and you are casually discussing coffee!'*

"Four sugars and just a drop of milk

for me," Herbert chipped in.

They drank their coffee then sat together on the sofa.

"Well, this is a rum do isn't it?" Herbert said quietly looking around the room.

"I was just thinking that myself a few minutes ago," Henry said, before adding: "I wonder what's on the telly?"

As it happened there was nothing, as when Herbert switched it on all he got was snow storm interference. "Maybe shit reception this far down," he muttered after flicking through a few channels and getting the same result.

Wanda, who had been sitting quietly, scanned the room carefully before getting up from the sofa and putting a forefinger against her lips, she made a soft 'shushing' sound.

"It's quite a nice suite really," she said loudly. "Could do with a bit of brightening up though, if I'm being honest." Henry and Herbert exchanged quick glances.

"Yes," she continued. "And there is a large bathroom just off the kitchen. Come and take a look Henry." Henry frowned lightly.

"Come and see Henry," she added, with an urgent sideways beckoning head movement. Henry frowned again, but followed her through to the kitchen and then into the bathroom. "Look," she said. "It's got a lovely large bathtub." Henry frowned again as she leaned forward and turned both taps on full.

"What the..." He managed, before she put her finger to her lips again, and whispered "Bugs." Henry frowned yet again.

"Bugs?" he said. She shushed him quietly.

"The suite might be bugged," she whispered in his ear. "I've seen enough James Bond movies to know that you can't take chances when you are in enemy territory."

"Oh, right," he whispered. "That's why you turned on the taps then!" She nodded.

"Yeah, they always do that, it buggers up the microphone or something." Henry nodded.

"What about cameras?" he said softly. She shook her head.

"Don't think so I had a good look around the lounge and there was no sign, and anyway cameras wouldn't tell them anything they'd be much more interested in talk."

"Better fill Herbert in then."

"Herbert!" She shouted. "Come and take a look at this lovely bathroom."

With Herbert in the loop and being relatively free of any video surveillance worries, they began a 'mute' bug search. It didn't take long to discover that the suite was infested with them.

They formed a close huddle in the bathroom. "We have to leave them where they are," Wanda whispered. "If we removed them and there was no feedback to whoever is doing the monitoring it will cause suspicion." Henry and Herbert nodded.

"So we just talk about the weather and other boring stuff then?" Henry whispered. Wanda shook her head.

"We can do more than that. We can bull this Sector up... Say how we admire the way Amon seems to be organising his sixty legions...Maybe we should even say how it's a pity that other Sectors are nowhere near as efficiently run..."

"And," Herbert whispered, "How about throwing in a little bit about how it's such a pity that Lucifer seems to be going a bit soft, buddying up to God, with the golf and such?"

"Ace!" Wanda said...to a duet of soft 'shushes'.

"Sorry," she whispered. "But we can't go over the top. It has to sound like snippets of, like, give away comment okay?" They both nodded.

For the next hour they concentrated on Henry's 'boring stuff', before dropping in some comments on how pleasing it was to see a Sector being so well run. That was followed by some more 'boring stuff', before Herbert said casually

"You know, going back to what we mentioned earlier, about how well Amon seems to be running things here; don't you think it's a pity that Lord Lucifer seems to be slacking off a bit?" Wanda stepped in quickly.

"Careful!" she said loudly. "If anybody else heard you saying that, you could find yourself in deep shit!"

"Look," he said evenly, "it was just between colleagues. And anyway, I was only saying what a lot of others are thinking..."

"Yes," Henry agreed. "I heard someone in Beelzebub's Sector mention how Lord Lucifer was even nipping up to Heaven every now and again for a game of golf!"

"Go on!" Herbert exclaimed.

"It's true!" And I bet that won't go down too well with the other Lords!"

Seeds planted, they then talked only 'boring stuff' for almost the next hour – included among which was their mission to attempt to solve the laundry problem that was plaguing Hell – before their chat was then interrupted by a heavy knocking on the front door.

"Lord Amon says you attend Him

now," the pitchfork wielding demon imperiously demanded.

***

Lord Amon was still dressed in his Roman General's armour, except for the golden, red plumed helmet, which removed and sat on his desk, revealed his blond closely cropped crew cut hair that stopped a mere two inches above eyebrows which framed a narrow pinched face that contained a long nose with flared nostrils, ice blue closely set eyes and thin, almost bloodless lips that were little more than a cruel gash above his chin.

His hands, with fingers loosely locked also rested on the desk's top and Henry noticed the fingers of both bore tattoos of a single word below the knuckle joints. The single word on each hand was '**HATE**'. He also noticed that the Lord's neck was inked with a large swastika on one side and a skull with a dagger through it on the other.

Amon looked Lord Lucifer's 'delegation' up and down coolly.

"You are here at Lucifer's command," he said, looking at Wanda. She noticed that he had dropped the 'Lord' and nodded.

"Yes Sir." He frowned.

"Address me as Lord Amon."

"Apologies... Lord Amon," she said meekly. He inclined his head.

"And your mission?"

"Lord Lucifer sent us to look into the problem with Hell's laundry service." As she said it she noticed a flicker of something cross his face. '*He knows that already* she thought.

"What laundry problem?" He said roughly. '*He's covering up the fact that he already knows*', she thought.

"For some time each Sector has been experiencing severe problems that are resulting in laundry services turning out clothes that are sub standard in terms of whiteness and general lack of cleanliness... Lord Amon."

"Laundry!" He shouted. "What the fuck do I care about fucking laundry! I'm not running a fucking After Dinner Club!"

"No, of course not Lord Amon. In fact my colleagues and I were only saying a short time ago how impressed we were with the professional way you seem to be running your Sector." The anger on his face slowly faded and the flinty ice gleam in his eyes seemed to soften slightly.

"Yes, I do run a tight Sector..."

"Indeed, we were privileged to witness your superb General ship out on the parade ground earlier Lord Amon. And did we not say earlier gentlemen," she turned to Henry and Herbert, "how it was a pity that some of the other Sectors were not as well managed." Henry and Herbert nodded firmly. Amon smiled thinly.

"And Lucifer; you know him well do you?"

"No not really Lord Amon, we were seconded from Purgatory to see if we could clear up the laundry problem..."

"Seconded by who?" Amon said with a slight narrowing of his eyes. *Seconded by whom, you thickko,* Wanda thought.

"Not sure Lord Amon, but quite possibly by God and Lord Lucifer..." Amon's eyes took on a flinty look again and the corners of his mouth twitched up slightly.

"By God and Lucifer," he said in a musing tone of voice. "That would be quite something wouldn't it?" Wanda was about to reply, but Henry butted in.

"What my colleague mentioned is merely gossip Lord Amon; we cannot really put any credence to it..."

"Credence? Amon said.

"We are not in a position to say it is true...Lord Amon." Amon nodded.

"And you were all in Purgatory then before you were se, se, picked for the mission?"

"Yes Lord Amon," Henry said softly.

"So you have no real allegiance to Lucifer?"

"No Lord Amon, no allegiance, either real or pretend. And, I probably shouldn't say this; but all three of us were not too pleased with Lord Lucifer when we were ordered to take on this mission."

"Not pleased why?"

"Well, Lord Amon we were all pretty settled in Purgatory and ... please don't take this the wrong way... but Hell is, well, pretty Hellish..."

Amon sat for a few seconds with his simian brow creased. *I can almost hear the rusty wheels clanking round inside that almost empty head,* Wanda thought.

"Very well," Amon said. "You may look into this laundry problem thing if you wish; but as far as I am concerned it is a load of bollocks."

They thanked him for taking time out of his busy schedule to speak with them and were then rewarded with an airy wave from a tattooed hand. They were dismissed.

Chapter 27

In the security of the S.E.L. they discussed the situation.

"He's certainly no Mensa candidate," Henry said. "But Nosy was right, he has street cunning. There's no way he's going to let anything of real value slip."

"I agree," Wanda said. "But you could be right in putting money on him Herbert. Did you notice how he was the only one who showed no respect for Lucifer by dropping the 'Lord' bit? And what about the look that crossed his ratty face when I mentioned the laundry problem the first time...he knew already, so he definitely has his finger on the pulse."

"Maybe that's just down to his suspicious nature," Henry said.

"Maybe," Wanda replied. "But then when I mentioned the thing about God and Lucifer working together, did you see how casually he took it, like it was no surprise? So maybe that Roman General complex and the battle training are a prelude to an upcoming coup attempt..." Herbert nodded.

"He's the best and probably, only candidate, so far and with only one to go, it looks to me like he is going to be our culprit."

"Well," Wanda said. "Strap yourselves in boys for the next and last stop, Level 500, Lord Asmodeus!"

***

The Super lift's door slid open to reveal that it had stopped directly opposite the entrance to another Reception Suite. This time the signing on the door modestly read:

Lord Asmodeus: Custodian of Hell's Loose Morals

Herbert "Hrumphed", Henry tutted loudly and Wanda smiled.

"Right," she said firmly, ditching the smile. "Let's see what we have here then!"

She pushed open the door and made a bee line for the resident bimbo clone.

"Good day, Tanith!" She said loudly. The blond bimbo (?) startled by the whirlwind entrance and by hearing her name spoken by a total stranger, didn't answer for a couple of seconds. When she did it was to say

"Who are you; what do you want here...and how do you know my name!"

Not a bimbo then, Wanda thought.

"I and my colleagues are special emissaries of Lord Lucifer. We seek audience with Lord Asmodeus...And we know your name, because we make it our business to know. I think that answers your questions, does it not?"

The receptionists hesitated to answer. Her initial inclination was to get up from her workstation, vault over it, and scratch this cocky bitch's eyes out. But a glance at the bitch's badge and specifically at Lord Lucifer's official sigil that it carried; stopped her in her tracks. Instead she took a slow deep breath.

"Yes madam, it does, thank you," she said, with each word seemingly drawn out of her by a pair of hot curling tongs.

Wanda inclined her head graciously in response to the obviously non-bimbo's climb down.

"Good," she said. "So would you please be so kind as to notify Lord Asmodeus of our arrival?"

"Certainly madam, if you would excuse me a moment I will just go and notify him."

Not phoning I see. Want to get a warning to him in private hey Wanda thought.

The receptionist rose, came round from her workstation and made her way over to a door at the far side of the room. She knocked lightly and then entered. A good three or four minutes went by before she came out and made her way back to the trio.

"Lord Asmodeus will see you now, please follow me." Wanda nodded.

"Thank you," she said pleasantly. "And by the way; just love those classy four inch heel, thigh length white boots."

Wanda led the way through the open door and her purposeful stride faltered ever so slightly when she saw a Greek God standing beside a desk.

He was tall. His short, slightly curled hair was almost ash blond. He had piercing blue eyes; and he might have been sculpted out of marble.

He was wearing a black short sleeved silk shirt that was open almost to the waist. His forearms and biceps were corded with muscle; while, what was on show of his pecs caused her to almost flick her tongue slowly over her lips.

She lowered her eyes to take in the tightly fitted cream slacks, the bulging thighs...and a third bulge that was situated in a much more interesting location. She swallowed slowly and raised her eyes.

"Lord Asmodeus I take it," she said just managing to kill a little squeak in her voice before it became too pronounced.

He smiled and nodded. "Indeed, and you are?" She cleared her throat.

"Wanda Wrigglesworth, Sir" she replied and immediately felt that she had uttered something very, very silly.

"I am here with my colleagues at the behest of Lord Lucifer," she added quickly, in an attempt to erase her previous words before they had time to reach his ears.

"So my receptionist informs me and the reason for the unannounced visit?" She swallowed again.

"It is in connection with a particular problem that has recently become apparent throughout all of Hell's Sectors..."

"And this particular problem is?"

"The laundry Sir..." She felt she had said something very, very silly again.

"By that I mean the fact that all Sectors have reported a marked deterioration in the quality of the end result in the laundering process..."

"The laundry is not cleaning the clothes properly?" He said with a slight smile and a tiny enquiring tilt of his head.

"Yes Sir. And my colleagues," she nodded towards Henry and Herbert, "are leading lights in the plumbing and detergent development fields."

"And your own area of expertise is?"

"I do not have any particular area of expertise Sir; I am merely a *Grade One Liaison Officer...*"

"And an *excellent Grade One Liaison Officer* I am sure," he said smoothly.

Henry noticed Wanda blush lightly and wasn't sure whether that was down to the compliment; or the fact that she had awarded herself a promotion.

"And you and your colleagues have visited the other Sectors in an effort to get to the bottom of the problem?"

"Yes Sir, we have."

"And these visits shed no light on the matter?"

"No Sir, and yours is the last Sector."

"Well we will have to give your esteemed colleagues our fullest cooperation then won't we?" Wanda nodded.

"Thank you Sir that would be very much appreciated." Asmodeus turned to Henry and Herbert.

"And you gentlemen; what do you need from me to assist your quest?" he said, directing his question at Henry.

"Well Sir I am sure that you are a very busy person; so perhaps you might direct us to your second in command, who can show us around your Sector, where we can scout for possible weak points in the water supply system?" Asmodeus nodded.

"It shall be done," he said smoothly before turning back to Wanda. "And while your expert colleagues are going about their business perhaps I could give you a personal guided tour of the Sector, followed, if you are amenable, by dinner?"

Henry frowned. Wanda blushed lightly then nodded.

"Excellent," Lord Asmodeus said as he picked up the phone on his desk and dialled a number. His call was answered almost immediately.

"Kobal," he said firmly, "It's me. Come round to my office immediately. I want you to take two gentlemen on a tour of the Sector's water utilities network.

"Yes Kobal, right now..." He put the phone down.

"My second in command Kobal will take you two gentlemen wherever you want to go. He will be here almost immediately." Thirty seconds later the nom-bimbo rapped lightly on the door and entered.

"Grand Demon Kobal," she said, stepping lightly aside as Asmodeus' number two crossed the threshold.

"Boss?" the red, horned and tailed demon (who was without a demon's usual pitchfork) said in a respectful voice.

"These gentlemen will tell you what they need. You will give them all the assistance they require." The demon nodded.

"Yes Boss," he said as he slowly backed out of the door. Tanith followed him and just as she was beginning to close the door, Asmodeus stopped her "Tanith," he said lightly, "A word please." She stepped outside, he followed and pulled the door closed. "I do not want to be disturbed until I give you a bell...you understand?" Tanith smiled.

"Oh yes Boss...I understand very well..." He nodded, opened the door and re-entered.

"Right gentlemen," he said adding a slight bow and a sweep of an arm. "Your guide awaits." Henry frowned lightly, thinking *what did Nosy say about him, wasn't it something about him being 'one horny bastard,' or something like that?*

Chapter 28

"Please take a seat," Asmodeus said. "Unless you are in a hurry for that tour of the Sector of course..."

"No Sir, no hurry."

"Good, and perhaps I can tempt you to a drink to help you unwind."

"Unwind Sir?" He shrugged lightly.

"You seem a little tense that's all."

"It's just been a hectic day Sir..."

"Well then," he said reaching into a drawer of his desk and bringing out a bottle of liquor, "We will have to iron out those uptight nerves then won't we"

As he placed the bottle on his desk she smoothed her skirt over her thighs and slid into a seat, while he retrieved two shot glasses from a cabinet.

"Hope whiskey neat will be okay," he said lightly, "I don't believe in spoiling good single malt with any sort of mixer." She smiled.

"Yes Sir, neat will be fine."

"Excellent...and by the way, while we are...alone...please refer to me by name; Sir seems a little stuffy don't you think?" He sat down opposite her, removed the screw top from the whiskey bottle and poured a good four fingers into each glass.

"Your good health, Wanda," he said smoothly as he picked up his glass.

"And yours S... Asmodeus," she replied picking up her own glass and clinking it against his.

Five minutes later he screwed the cap back on the whiskey bottle, rose from his seat, moved round to her side of the desk, pulled her gently to her feet, swept the desk clear of bottle, empty glasses, telephone and papers and bent her backwards onto the desk top; legs up in the air.

***

"I hope she will be alright," Henry murmured to Herbert as they followed Grand Demon Kobal to the inter-level lift.

"I wouldn't worry too much about *Grade One* Liaison Officer Wrigglesworth, if I was you, Henry." Herbert said dryly. "I think she knows what she is doing..."

"Well," Henry said quietly, "while she's doing her thing, I guess we should do our bit by trying to get something out of our friend, Kobal."

"The Sector's incoming water supply treatment room is forty levels down," Kobal said as he reached out and pressed a button. Henry nodded.

"I seem to be spending half my death in lifts these days," He said conversationally as they began to descend. "And tell me, Grand Demon Kobal... is it alright if I address you that way, by the way?" Kobal nodded.

"That is my title," Henry returned his nod.

"Good; tell me then, have you served Lord Asmodeus long?"

"As his Grand Demon, for just short of one thousand years..."

"That long...and before that, you came up through the ranks did you?"

"Yes."

"And what about Lord Lucifer?" Henry said to Kobal's back... and smiled to himself as he noticed a sudden tensing in the Grand Demon's shoulders.

"Lord Lucifer?" Kobal said lightly. "What about Lord Lucifer?"

"Oh, I was just wondering how Lord Asmodeus got on with Lord Lucifer, that's all." *There it was again; that tensing of the shoulders!*

"I could not say, Lord Asmodeus does not talk to me about his relationships."

Liar, Liar, pants on fire! Henry thought, before mentally patting himself on the back for his brilliant interrogation technique.

The lift came to a halt and when the door opened they found themselves in a large high ceilinged room that hummed with machinery. "The main water treatment and pumping room," Kobal said.

"Excellent," Henry said in his best professional voice. "This then is my colleague's area of expertise so perhaps we could leave him to it?" Kobal frowned.

"Leave him to it?"

"Yes, is there somewhere around where we could grab a coffee or something? It would give me a chance to learn a little more about what a Grand Demon does."

"Why?"

"Why? Well I must confess to a fascination about the hierarchy in Hell. There seems to be so many different levels. And with Grand Demon being such a senior position I thought you would be the best person, or rather Demon to ask." The Grand Demon's eyes narrowed slightly.

"How long have you been a resident here?" Henry feigned surprise.

"A resident? Oh hell no; my colleagues and I were seconded from Purgatory and so I am rather ignorant when it comes to Hell's make up!"

"Who seconded you?"

"Lord Lucifer, I suppose..."

"So you did not come direct from

Lucifer? *Ah, so you also drop the 'Lord' from the title!* Henry thought.

"Good He...Hell no! In fact to tell you the truth we were pretty pissed off. I mean Purgatory is no picnic, but we were all used to death there. And I know I shouldn't say this...but we all cursed Lord Lucifer for having us dragged down to Hell."

"So you owe no allegiance to Lucifer?" *There he goes again!* Henry thought.

"No, none...Does that shock you?" Grand Demon, Kobal shrugged lightly.

"There is a Sector cafe three levels up." He said flatly.

"Excellent! I'll just tell my colleague where we are going and he can join us there when he has finished his examination."

Henry strolled over to Herbert who was busy looking professional by tapping on pipes and listening closely to gurgling sounds.

"Kobal could be in on it with Asmodeus," Henry said quietly after glancing back in the Grand Demon's direction.

"Why, what makes you think that?"

"Tell you later..." Henry whispered. "We are just going up three levels for a coffee," he added loudly. "Join us there if you can't find anything here."

***

"Cheers," Henry said brightly as he lifted the cup to his lips and took a sip. "Mmm, this is good coffee," he said. "Does it come from this Sector, or do you have it shipped in?"

"Couldn't say."

"Oh, anyway, it sure beats the crap that passes for coffee up in Purgatory!"

"Oh right; then maybe you should put in a transfer request to come down here permanently then..." Henry grinned.

"Nice one, Kobal...you don't mind if I call you Kobal, do you?" The Grand Demon shrugged.

"Good, I wouldn't like you to think I was being disrespectful or anything. Anyway, like I was saying earlier, I'm interested in how things work down here. You really must tell me a little more about what a Grand Demon does..."

A half hour and three more cups of coffee later, Herbert appeared.

"Any luck?" Henry asked as Herbert approached their table.

"No nothing. I thought there might have been a problem with the seals on one of the reticulating pumps, but it turned out to be okay..."

"Oh well, pull up a chair and I will go and get you a coffee. We've been having a good chat about Grand Demon Kobal's work down here...fascinating stuff..."

Henry came back with three coffees on a tray. "It's free," he said with a grin. "All I had to do was flash Lord Lucifer's sigil on my badge; perhaps I should have ordered us a chilli con carne as well!" Herbert threw him a sour look.

"Coffee is fine," he said sweetly. Henry smiled.

"I was telling Kobal – he doesn't mind me calling him by name by the way – about how we were not impressed by Lord Lucifer seconding us from Purgatory and how we were pretty pissed off with him."

"Oh right; and did you mention anything about him and God buddying up?" Herbert said casually.

"What, about them playing golf together, you mean?" Henry said, looking sideways for a surprised reaction...that didn't come; until a belated snort from Kobal was followed by "Maybe there's a particular Lord heading for a dollop of shit..." Henry and Herbert exchanged quick glances.

"That Lord, perhaps, being Lord Lucifer?" Henry said casually. Kobal smiled, but didn't reply.

"I wouldn't be surprised!" Herbert butted in. "If I was one of the other Lords I'd be pretty pissed if the Boss started going soft!" The Grand Demon nodded slowly.

"There is some unrest...but you didn't hear that from me, right?"

"Mum's the word," Herbert said and followed it up with a zipping motion across his lips.

"Well," Henry said two minutes later as he drained his cup, "where to now Herbert?"

"Back up to Lord Asmodeus I suppose as it looks like we've drawn a total blank on the laundry problem."

They made a show of thanking Kobal for his time and left him in the cafe.

"Well," Henry said as they made their way back to the lift. "I don't think there's much doubt about our potential culprits is there?"

"No, but any doubt is a bit too much don't you think?"

"What more could we do Herbert? Amon and Asmodeus are not likely to say 'fair cop guv'ners' are they?"

"No, suppose not. So, are we finished down here then?"

"Yes, let's get back, pick up Wanda and get the Hell out of it..."

***

The lift door sighed open and they stepped out into the reception room; just in time to see the door to Asmodeus' office open and an oddly unsteady Wanda come out. Henry frowned and thought *what's up with her legs, she looks a little bit bandy!* A second later a grinning Asmodeus followed her and gave her bum a playful goosing! Cue: a sharp intake of breath from Henry and a guilty look from Wanda as she saw Henry's gobsmacked face.

After a silent walk back to the visitor's suite Herbert made himself scarce by going to the toilet to 'freshen up', leaving Henry and Wanda in the lounge.

"I'm sorry Henry," Wanda said slowly as soon as Herbert had disappeared. "I mean, you're a lovely man; but really I have a weakness for mostly, men with power. Two premier league football managers, the Chief Executive of a multi-national corporation, a top Hedge Fund manager and a kebab shop owner were some of my 'minor indiscretions.'" Henry blinked and shook his head.

"I don't understand," he said slowly. "A kebab shop owner?"

"Well I did say 'mostly' men with power. And you are right, that one was a big mistake. His wife caught us at it and she nearly filleted me with a bloody boning knife!"

"So that's how you came to end up in

Purgatory then?"

"Yes, pretty much...oh yes, plus I suppose a spell in jail for perverting the course of justice when I perjured myself giving the Hedge Fund manager a wonky alibi didn't help..."

"No, don't suppose it did," Henry muttered gloomily. He was on a real downer. One minute death was not so bad; he'd found his old childhood girlfriend and they had 'got it on' as the parlance goes. But then the next minute, there she was having it rumpy-pumpy with one of Hell's big knob – he wondered if he actually was hung like a bull elephant – Lords!

"I know you are very disappointed," Wanda said, noticing his face. "But really we only just met again after all those years; and we were just kids way back then behind that bike shed..." Henry nodded.

"It's just that I have never really had what you could call a steady girlfriend and when we met up again in Purgatory it was like...like... it was somehow meant to be..."

"Yes I know; and it was lovely seeing you again Henry. And we have had quite an adventure together, haven't we?" Henry sighed.

"Yes, it's just a pity that we haven't exactly managed to get what we went for." He was on the verge of adding: *well I didn't anyway*; but his innate sense of chivalry stopped him.

"Well," Wanda said slowly, "I think you could be wrong there Henry..." Henry frowned.

"Why, why am I wrong?" Wanda bit her lip lightly.

"Wellll...While he was like coming up to a critical moment...so to speak...he did sort of yell out..."

"Yell out?"

"Yes, he yelled out '*And you're the next one who I'm going to fuck Lucifer!*'"

"Was that all?" Wanda nodded.

"Until he went '*Aaahhh!*' or, something like that anyway." Henry took a deep breath.

"Well, it looks like he could be the ringleader alright; but is that enough evidence; a demon on the verge who shouts out a macho statement?"

"What, like "*And you're the next one I'm going to fuck Lucifer!*' I would say that was a pretty conclusive statement, wouldn't you?"

"True, but, would it hold up in court?" Wanda shook her head slowly.

"In court...what court...the Court of Lucifer? I don't think the Arch Demon is going to be too worried by such niceties as *Proof Absolute*, do you?"

"Maybe not. But we've not talking about a parking offence or some similar misdemeanour here are we? We're talking about something that could determine a Hell of a lot more aren't we?" Wanda nodded slowly.

"Okay, but what more do we need?"

"You will have to, er, get him to do the deed again, but this time he'll need to give you more..."

"More," she said with the trace of a wistful look on her face, "He gave me quite a lot last time..." Henry noticed the look and sighed as an image of a bull elephant lumbered across the panoramic screen in his mind.

He sighed again then shrugged lightly. His romantic dream was over. Wanda was not to be 'the one' and Henry Pratt's poxy life had had the last laugh by following him into poxy death...

He squared his narrow shoulders, raised his chin an inch and nodded. *Death*, he suddenly thought, *has somehow sharpened my mind; so okay, if that is how it is going to be, then no wallowing. Sod life and sod fucking death, I will just...*His thoughts were then interrupted by someone speaking. It was Wanda.

"Pardon?" he said.

"I said right, I'm prepared to take another for the team..." Henry even managed a thin smile.

Herbert whistled when they told him

about Wanda's earlier 'sacrifice' for the cause.

"So," he said brightly. "Asmodeus is the culprit hey? Boy I would hate to be in his shoes when his Boss gets his claws into him!"

"Ah well," Henry said. "We need a little more proof before we go back to Head Office."

"More proof?"

"Yes; Wanda has agreed to, er, see if she can get a little more out of him by, er, using her womanly wiles..."

Using her womanly wiles, Herbert thought, *typical Henry speak*. He glanced across at Wanda who was somehow standing it seemed to him, with her legs slightly bowed.

"So what more do you need from him Wanda, if that is not too indelicate a question?"

"Whatever I can get," she replied. Herbert nodded then thought *and looking at the way you are stood, I bet that's bloody plenty!*

"Right," Henry said. "The best course of action is for you to think of a pretext to get back into his living quarters...er, I take it that was where you...you know..."

"No, actually it was in his office..."

"In his office?"

"Er, yes...over his desk actually... if you really want to know." Henry closed his eyes for a second.

"Over his desk...Right well...Whatever. You need to get back there for an encore," he said flatly. Wanda frowned.

"Listen Henry," she said quietly. "I'm a grown woman and I don't appreciate you talking to me like I'm some sort of tramp." Henry nodded.

"Apologies," he said softly. "You are right, that was uncalled for. I guess I'm still feeling a bit...raw."

"Thank you, apology accepted," Wanda replied a little coolly.

"Ah!" Herbert said wading in with his size tens. "You two not an item any more then?" Henry took a deep breath.

"No Herbert; but the three of us are still a team and we need to wrap this thing up as quickly as we can and get back topside with our report."

***

Early next morning Henry awoke in his single bed and made his way into the kitchen to check the fridge for breakfast makings. He found some eggs, which he cracked into a basin and whisked up with a large spoon ready to make three omelettes. He then switched the percolator on before tapping lightly on Wanda's and Herbert's bedroom doors.

Wanda arrived at the breakfast table first and after a brief "Sleep well?" "Yes, you?" "Yes thank you." They sat down together... but at least half a mile apart. The awkward silence was then broken by a still half asleep Herbert who strolled in scratching his head and yawning.

"Morning campers," he said and in return got two weak smiles.

They finished the omelettes and drank their coffee and Herbert got the ball rolling with, "Okay, so what next?" Henry looked at Wanda. Wanda took a deep breath.

"Well," she said in a business like voice, "He..." Henry interrupted.

"Who, Asmodeus?" Wanda's mouth hardened a little.

"Yes, Asmodeus. He said he would show me around the Sector and then take me to dinner..."

"Oh, right, but you never got round to that bit though..." She shot him a 'look'.

"No we didn't get round to that bit Henry because he was too busy rogering me silly!"

Henry looking a little abashed said "Sorry... still a bit raw..." Wanda sniffed.

"Right; so I think I should take him up on the dinner offer; but make it lunch instead and then afterwards...suggest that maybe we could go back to his place..."

"What, not the office and the desk again?" Henry chimed in. Wanda took another deep breath.

"No, not the office desk again Henry. This time if I am going to lay back and think of England I want to do it in comfort and not sprawled across a fucking desk with my legs in the air!"

"Sorry... Sorry..."

***

"Good morning Tanith," Wanda said brightly. Tanith smiled a smile that said: *He gave it to you big time didn't he, cocky bitch!*

"Is Lord Asmodeus in his office yet?" Another smile.

"Yes madam he is, is he expecting you?"

"No, not really." A smile, bordering on a grin.

"No problem, you obviously get on very well, just go straight in."

"Thank you Tanith."

"No problem madam."

Wanda strolled over to his office, opened the door and froze. The first thing she saw was his gorgeous bare buttocks. The second thing she saw was a pair of white thigh length, four inch heel leather boots draped over his shoulders.

He turned around and while carrying on with his pounding said, "Good morning Wanda, I'll be with you in a minute or two..."

"Don't bother," she said coldly. "Take as long as you want..." She spun on her heels and head high, made her way out of the office past a grinning Tanith.

"That must have been a real quicky!" Herbert said as the slamming of the guest suite door announced her return. Henry gave him a sour look.

"What happened?" he said as he noticed the stony look on her face.

"He was otherwise engaged."

"Otherwise engaged?"

"Let's just leave it at that shall we..." Herbert smiled thinly, said "Ahh," very softly; then thought: *A woman scorned, or rather a woman who has just caught her man (or demon) in the act of going jiggy-jig with someone else!* Henry was still confused.

"So he was somewhere else other than in his office then?" Wanda's eyes narrowed and her mouth opened a little about to give him both barrels.

"Er, I think it best if you leave it," Herbert said to Henry. "And I think we should forget about *Assignation Part Two,* too."

"Thank you Herbert," she said. "And I think we should get the fuck out of this glorified knocking shop now."

**

They were half way back to Home Base before the reason for Wanda's permanent stone face and stubborn silence finally dawned on Henry.

She must have caught him at it! He thought. But then that thought was quickly followed by another. *But why should that annoy her so much? It wasn't as though he was her husband, or that they were a steady item or something?*

He shook his head. *Women!* The little voice then added, with its own shake of the head; before carrying on with: *Or rather it should be Woe-men; 'cause that's what they can end up giving you...*

Chapter 29

Nosy took them for a long and thorough de-briefing, before placing them in what he termed 'protective custody'.

"It will only be for a day or so until I can get the tapes typed up and presented to the Boss; who, no doubt will want to see you personally to go over some of it again."

Thirty-six hours later they were released from 'pokey' and on their way up to Head Office.

"What do you think He will say?" Henry said. Herbert shrugged.

"Probably be a bit pissed off because we didn't get more in the way of proof..." Henry's face dropped.

"You don't think He will be a bit extra pissed do you?"

"Extra pissed?"

"Yes, while I was down there I did keep my eyes open for anything to do with the laundry problem...but no luck there."

"I wouldn't worry about that squire; I think He has other more important things on His mind, don't you?"

"Yes, I suppose so...but problems with the laundry are no joke you know."

"Yeah, well, we are about to find out

what kind of mood He is in just now aren't we?"

Nosy opened the door to Reception and ushered the three of them in, where they were welcomed by Joan.

"Nice to see you back," she said. "The Big Three are waiting for you."

"Big Three?" Henry said nervously.

"Yes, The Boss, His Son and Lord Lucifer..." Henry swallowed.

"The Devil is here too!" Joan nodded.

"Yes, but as a matter of courtesy, if he addresses you, please don't use that term, he much prefers Lord Lucifer," she said casually as she picked up the phone.

"They are here Sir, shall I send them in?" There was a single bass word response of "Yes" and ten seconds later they were standing in front of 'The Big Three,' who were sitting around the large desk.

"Welcome back," Jesus said warmly. "Please take a seat and we will get down to business." Henry, although still 'heaven struck' in the presence of God and His Son, focussed his eyes on the Arch Demon, who was looking, he had to admit, rather handsome. *Odd*, he thought. *He doesn't look like I imagined. Where's his horns, his little goatee beard, his red eyes and his barbed tail?* The little voice in his head, tutted. *Bloody Hell, Henry, that description is out of the Ark and was put about by the Church to scare the shit out of everyone!*

Henry nodded to himself and moved his attention to Jesus.

"First of all, We would like to thank you for your efforts," Jesus said. "And although you were not able to bring back conclusive proof of a potential coup, Lord Lucifer is of a mind that what you did discover was enough to prove to him that his initial doubts have been put to bed." He then turned to Lucifer, who nodded firmly.

"So," Jesus continued. "We have brought you here to discuss any points that Lord Lucifer feels the need to clarify. Over to you Lord Lucifer."

Lucifer inclined his head in Jesus' direction and thanked Him before turning towards the trio who were sat hands on laps next to Nosy Parker.

"Right," he said. "I just want to be sure on a few points. You are all three in agreement that none of the other Lords gave cause for concern, apart from Asmodeus and Amon?" All three nodded firmly and Wanda then put her hand up.

"If I might be spokesperson Sir?" Lucifer nodded.

"We were not able to get conclusive proof Sir, but to be honest that was surely a long shot." Lucifer nodded again.

"Granted."

"But all three of us were forcefully struck by the attitudes of Lord's Amon and Asmodeus, once they thought that we were very much Anti-Lucifer, if you will excuse the term." Lucifer smiled lightly. "Then they both openly expressed similar dislike for you Sir."

"Expressed how?"

"Well Sir, Lord Amon, was frankly scathing when he mentioned your name and even when he did that he refused to give you your due title, referring to you as 'Lucifer' only."

"Was that the only indication?"

"Well, in speech, yes Sir, but when my colleague spoke about you 'buddying up with God'; playing golf and such. I noted, not surprise, but a particular nasty gleam in his eyes."

"Right, anything else?"

"No Sir, just common agreement between us that he stood out as the only candidate up to that point. Oh, and perhaps the fact that we found him engaged in bloody manoeuvres with his legions. And that he puts them all through their paces two of three times every week; which to us was perhaps a sign that he was readying them for something more than manoeuvres." Lucifer nodded slowly.

"And Asmodeus?" Wanda blushed lightly.

"Well Sir, there was nothing concrete until...until we got together, if I may put it that way..."

"You may; and in my experience when humans or devils 'get together' there are often words or actions that are revealing."

"Yes, thank you Sir. Well when he was at an, hmm, crucial point so to speak, he said something that was quite damning..."

"And this damning statement was?" Wanda blushed again and she swallowed.

"He said, "*And you're the next one I am going to fuck Lucifer,*" Sir."

"Did he indeed. And was there anything else?"

"Not directly from him Sir, other than the fact that, like Amon, he was scathing when he mentioned you by name.

"The other hint came when my colleagues were in discussion with his second in command..."

"Grand Demon, Kobol you mean?"

"Yes Sir."

"And what did he say?"

"He said that 'Some Demons were soon going to cop a load of shit', or words to that effect. He also said that there was unrest afoot."

"Thank you madam," Lucifer said

before he turned his attention back to God and His Son.

"Your agents are to be congratulated as in the circumstances they did even better than I had thought possible." God nodded.

"And what, if I may ask, are your next actions going to be?"

"I will call a meeting of the Lords immediately to discuss a radical restructuring of the command echelon and while they are chewing that over and wondering who is for the chop I will confront the two Lords..."

"And then?"

"And then they will deny everything of course."

"And what then?"

"And then I will listen to their protestations..."

"And then?"

"And then...they will be very, very sorry that they had the temerity to even think that they could usurp Me!"

Chapter 30

Lord Lucifer smiled lightly as he picked up the foot high heavy figurine bookends one in each hand and strode over to the shelf which carried his small library that lay in three little piles.

He plonked the bookends, one at each end of the shelf, then took down the books, placed them on a nearby table and picked up a yellow duster and one of the tomes. He glanced at its title, *The Satanic Bible;* nodded and gave it a good dusting.

He picked up the next, *The Devil's Dictionary* and dusted that also. He did the same with *The Art of War; The Black Pullet; Ars Notoria; Al-Jiwah; Pseudomonarchia Daedonum; The Necronomicon* and *Golf for Beginners.*

He then carried them two at a time back over to the shelf where he lined them up neatly according to size; and satisfied, nodded and smiled again.

He picked up the left hand figurine and slid it up to *The Satanic Bible*, noting as he did so the angry look on the figure's face and the clenched fists with the word '**HATE**' tattooed across them.

He smiled again as he slid the right

hand bookend into place; noting with pleasure the look of absolute shock on the other figure's face.

"I had originally thought of pot plants for the conservatory," he mused, looking directly at his new book ends. "And I've heard it said that talking to plants can be very beneficial in helping them attain healthy growth; but in this particular case that would hardly be appropriate now, would it?

"Anyway pot plants only have a very limited shelf life don't they and this way I can get pleasure from looking at you occasionally for, oh, a thousand years at the very least..."

Chapter 31

"But what about the laundry problem Sir, I didn't manage to tackle that?" God smiled and shook His head.

"Oh that's no problem at all Henry. All I have to do is click my fingers and that particular problem will disappear." Henry goggled.

"How Sir?"

"You have a chemistry degree I believe?" Henry nodded slowly.

"Yes Sir, but why bring that up?"

"Well as the Creator, I'm pretty clued up on any number of subjects you know..."

"Well, yes Sir I suppose You would be..."

"One of the things I am clued up on Henry is chemistry. Now you obviously know which molecules combine to make water."

"Of course Sir; Hydrogen and Oxygen..."

"Correct so all I had to do was smuggle a rogue molecule or two into the non-drinking water supply which comes from the *River Styx* to change its make-up." Henry nodded slowly.

"So, what did you use Sir?" In answer God said,

"Henry; tell me did you notice anything slightly peculiar about the clothes down there?" Henry pursed his lips in thought.

"Well, now You mention it Sir, once or twice I think I caught a very faint whiff of...rotten eggs?"

"Excellent Henry. Rotten eggs...So?"

"Hydrogen Sulphide!" Henry exclaimed. God beamed then Henry suddenly frowned.

"But hydrogen sulphide is poisonous!"

"Indeed, but it was in the non-drinking water; and I did modify it to lessen any dramatic impact, such as death... again."

"So...If You didn't need me to track down the problem, You really didn't have any need to put that bloody – sorry – great tree smack in front of me then!"

"*Au contraire*, Henry. I suspected that something was going on down there from the last report sent by our agent and because Lucy and I had a pact that neither of us should directly meddle in the other's business, I needed to employ a less direct plan of action... for the greater good...you understand."

"Well, yes Sir I can see how You would take that stand..."

"Right so what was called for was the introduction of someone with the right credentials who would have *carte blanche* to move around down there to tackle the laundry problem without any interference."

"The laundry problem that You had engineered." God nodded.

"Granted; and during which he or she could do some snooping." Henry took a deep breath.

"Okay Sir, I understand that, sort of; but I did have some 37 years of life left to me..." God nodded.

"Yes My son. And I am quite prepared to give you back those years."

"You are!"

"Of course. You were called before your time and did have another 37 years or so left. So it is only right that you should get them back. What you do with them is down to free will of course, so who knows, you may even become a bloodthirsty murderer come rapist. In which case your odds of getting back up here would be rather dramatically diminished."

"So You will send me back. How?" God tutted.

"Really Henry, I am The Supreme One!"

"Oh, right, of course. So, it would be like I have been spending a...a... a Holiday from Hell, I suppose then?" God smiled.

"Well, if you want to put it that way." Henry nodded.

"So, You click Your fingers or whatever, and I reappear when and where?"

"At the precise moment you were, um, called."

"And what about that bloody...sorry, what about that tree?"

"There will be no tree."

"Thank G...thank You! Wow I'll have some story to tell when I get back!" God shook his head slowly.

"No my son, your memory of everything that happened after your contact with that tree will be wiped for your own good. You babbling on to all and sundry about your marvellous adventure – *or Holiday from Hell, as you put it* – would only end up with you in the loony bin...and that would be a waste of your remaining years, would it not?"

"Well...yes Sir, You're right. I guess I was just getting a little carried away seeing as I have spent all my life until You sent for me pretty much as a nobody..." God shook His head.

"Henry Pratt," He said, "You are not a no-body. Were you not hurtling down a fearsome snow slope when, ahem, you encountered that tree?"

"Well, yes Sir, but I was trying to back off at the time..."

"Irrelevant. What was your last statement as you hurtled down that fearsome slope?" Henry stroked his chin.

"Not sure Sir...Oh wait a minute; yes, I remember! I said, or rather screamed: 'You can do this'". God nodded.

"Now concentrate on those words my son and understand that they are not the words of a no-body....*Bon voyage...*" Henry held a hand up quickly.

"Just a moment Sir!"

"I thought you were in a hurry to get back down to the 'Vale of Tears', Henry."

"Well, yes Sir, but I would like to say my goodbyes first; if that is alright with You?"

"Of course, how remiss of Me! You have one hour and then you will be automatically transported back to earth."

***

Henry made a beeline for *The Angel* and was relieved to find Herbert and Wanda sitting at a table in a quiet corner.

"Where've you been?" Herbert said, "We have been sat here for over an hour."

"I got a call from The Boss!"

"Really! Guess you were chuffed about that then hey."

"Yes, of course. But you'll never guess what He told me!"

"You're right squire, but hold on a minute while I get you a bevy," Herbert said as he got to his feet and made his way over to the bar. Henry glanced at his watch.

Herbert returned after two minutes and pushed the glass of Harp lager over to Henry, who picked it up, said "Cheers, and this is my last drink up here in Heaven!"

Wanda blinked. "Your last drink, why?" Henry glanced at his watch again.

"Because in about three minutes I am going to be whisked back down to earth, to resume my life!"

"What?" Herbert said. "You mean The Boss is actually sending you back! Bloody Hell, that must be a first!"

Henry nodded. "Probably; but I wanted to come here first to say my goodbyes. You've been a good friend to me Herbert and I am going to miss you," Henry said softly with the hint of a catch in his voice.

"Hey!" Herbert said, "Stop that or you'll have me blubbing! And anyway you'll be back again in 37 or so years won't you?"

"Yes, but The Boss told me that I will have every memory of up here wiped out when He sends me back. So I won't know you when I do return..."

"Well then, I'll still be on the turnstile and I will keep an eye out for you and we can become mates again!" Henry smiled.

"That would be great Herbert and I will look forward to meeting you again...for the first time." He then turned to Wanda.

"And I am going to miss you too Wanda," he said softly.

"What, even though I let you down badly," she said quietly with her head slightly bowed. Henry smiled.

"Of course, we were a team weren't we! And although it didn't work out like I would have wanted it to, I will miss you too. So," he said softly. "Would it be okay if I gave you a goodbye kiss?" Wanda's eyes misted up as he leaned forward and their lips met, just before he blinked out of existence.

Chapter 32

"You can do this!" He screamed at the wind that was threatening to tear his goggles and nose off his face. "You can do this!" And somehow he did. His mad headlong *Mach III* plunge down the killer 78% (to him almost perpendicular) slope, suddenly slowed to *Mach I*, then to a mere 100 miles per hour, before the ground levelled out and heart pounding, knees knocking, he glided serenely to a stop twenty yards in front of a large timber ski lodge.

He raised a shaking gloved hand and wiped it across his misted goggles.

"The tree," he muttered. "I'm sure there was a bloody great tree that leapt right out in front of me*!" There are no bloody great trees in the middle of Austria's steepest ski slope, you numpty,* his brain said in a tsk tsk, head shaking voice. "Of course not," he muttered. "It must have been some sort of mad vision conjured up out of panic..."

He wiped his goggles again before lifting them up onto his forehead and passing a still shaking hand across his brow. He took a long deep breath and as he began to slowly exhale he heard someone shout "Bravo!"

The man and woman were standing in the open door of the ski lodge and they were applauding! Henry waved, they waved back. Henry said "Good afternoon." And the man said back "English?" Henry nodded and clumped his way over to the lodge.

"Bravo!" the man said again slapping him on his back.

"I never see such fast descent of *The Harakiri*! Most times people slalom, at least a little; but you come straight down like you being bat out of Hell!" Henry frowned lightly. *A bat out of Hell*, he thought. *Strange those words seem to somehow resonate.* He shook his head then shrugged lightly and swallowed.

"Er well, the beast was there to be tamed," he said. "So I decided to give it the respect it was due by giving it my best..."

***

Henry took his seat on the little plane and removed an A5 sized brown manila envelope from the inside pocket of his jacket. He opened the flap and slid out a glossy coloured print that showed a group of six grinning people, standing three either side of a slightly built early middle aged man.

All six were pointing towards the man who was wearing a black tee shirt emblazoned with flame red printing that shouted: *'I Survived The Harakiri'*.

The man had his right wrist bent and forefinger pointing to the wording that ran across his puffed out chest. He had a faint, almost smug smile on his face.

Henry carefully slid the photo back into the envelope and placed it gently back into his inside pocket ... where it lay up against a glossy brochure that was headlined *'Harakiri: The Perfect Thrill.*

He fastened his seatbelt nodded and said softly, "I'm quite looking forward to getting back to work."

Greetings dear reader! I hope you enjoyed the story, and if you did I would really appreciate a short (or long!) review on Amazon.

The story itself began life a few years ago as a three episode mini - series titled *Heaven, Purgatory, Hell,* written for television for Ronnie Barker and Ronnie Corbett's *The Two Ronnies* programme.

The manuscript was sent off and instead of the usual 7-10 day return, several weeks went by before the 'dreaded thud' on the doormat announced its unwelcome homecoming.

Instead of a bog standard rejection slip a 'nice' letter came with the package. It 'thanked me for 'the effort/work that I had put into it' and also said that 'serious consideration had been given to taking it up...but due to circumstances beyond their control (that would soon become apparent) it could not be used.'

Two weeks later Ronnie Barker announced his retirement and the manuscript was shoved into a drawer (that was then forcefully slammed shut).

Tempus, as is its wont, *fugited* and I had occasion to open that draw for something or other and saw the manuscript lying there. I took it out and metaphorically dusted it off. Should I go back to it and perhaps re-write it

as a novel I thought. Well obviously I
did...So again, if you enjoyed it...etc, etc.

In conclusion may I most sincerely
state here that if any reader has found
themselves to be outraged and or disgusted
by what they consider irreligious or
blasphemous content....well, as The Boss said
on page 72, 'Tough Titty...'

Peter Clayfield
Manchester, England

P.S. A Shameless plug:

Henry's Holiday from Hell is one of five novels
of mine on Amazon. The other four are:

Dog Day Dimp: a black humour offering that
features the trials, tribulations and minor
triumphs of one-armed dwarf, David Ignatius
Montgomery Parker (DIMP for short).

About the only thing Davey has going
for him – apart from an almost uncanny
ability to attract the ball to his face while
playing in goal for a local five-a-side football
team –   is an outsized penis. This
unfortunately is something of a double-edged
sword, as every time he entertains naughty

thoughts, the rush of blood into his tool
causes him to faint from light-headedness.

Abyss of Time:
Is a murder chase through time that includes
vicious Sunsail Pirates, Power Towers,
Rastafarian Bob Marley worshippers and
Mutants.

The novel contains a rather graphic
rape/murder scene that precipitates the
chase.

The actual science fiction content is
minimal and is restricted to the transference
into a future world that is recovering from an
atomic holocaust. Rather, it majors on the
three main characters – rapist/murderer,
Tibor Varkas; the victim's husband, Damon
Carter-Brown; and her brother, Quintino
Orion – and the psychological changes on
them that are brought about through the
transference.

The Land of Lost Content:
Is based on an actual event, when in 1631,
Barbary Pirates raided an Irish fishing village
and kidnapped over 100 villagers, included
among whom were young lovers Erin
O'Connor and James Pallow; and took them
to Algiers to be sold in the slave markets.
The lovers are separated. She is transported
to the Constantinople harem of sadistic

Sultan, Murad IV where she must learn new skills, including training in the erotic arts; while James is taken to a slave labour camp. Can he somehow escape and rescue her? And can they somehow return to Ireland and bring the shadowy figure behind the villager's abduction to justice?

Ingane-ye-Sipepo, Child of Storm:
Is, like the novel above, a Drama/Romance offering. It begins in a 19th Century Manchester mining village, moves to the Zululand sugar cane fields where the heroine, Sarah Wilson, is given the Zulu name Ingane-ye-Sipepo, *Child of Storm:* and climaxes after the avoidable and ultimately bloody, Zulu War.

P.P.S.
While I am at it I might as well mention:

Shades of Twilight, Black Night, Lucid Dawn:
A collection of poems dedicated to those who have set aside a little corner of their hearts for events joyous, sad or tragic.

Shadow Warriors:
A look back at of some of the boxing heroes (and villains) whose careers have, perhaps, faded from the memory of today's 'average' fight fan.

Made in the USA
Charleston, SC
17 December 2016